hearing
God's
voice

hearing
God's
voice

Eight keys to connecting with God

VERN HEIDEBRECHT

victor®
The Bible Teacher's Teacher

COOK COMMUNICATIONS MINISTRIES
Colorado Springs, Colorado • Paris, Ontario
KINGSWAY COMMUNICATIONS LTD
Eastbourne, England

Victor® is an imprint of
Cook Communications Ministries, Colorado Springs, CO 80918
Cook Communications, Paris, Ontario
Kingsway Communications, Eastbourne, England

Hearing God's Voice
© 2007 by Vern Heidebrecht

Published in association with the literary agency of Les Stobbe, 300 Doubleday Rd., Tryon, NC 28782.

First Printing, 2007
Printed in the United States
1 2 3 4 5 6 7 8 9 10 Printing/Year 11 10 09 08 07

ISBN 978-0-7814-4481-1

Dedication

I DEDICATE THIS BOOK TO MY WIFE CAROL, AND OUR FAMILY: Murray & Holly, Bob & JoAnn, Dave & Michelle, Karla & Menno. Carol has been my partner in ministry for over 43 years. She has often helped me discern the voice of God in our lives. I also thank our family for their encouragement and support throughout the process of writing this book.

I am grateful for the many who have been an encouragement to me during this project, especially my assistant, Delaine Moon, and readers Susan Anquist and Jim Coggins.

I want to give a special tribute to the Spirit-filled people of Northview Community Church whose love, prayers, and encouragement have made ministry a reality for Carol and me.

Contents

Preface

THE WORLD SHOUTS AND SHOVES TO GET OUR ATTENTION. WE ARE bludgeoned with the onslaught of sales pitches and success schemes. Often we feel exhausted and worn out. But the spiritual world is different. Our God does not assault us. Rather, he invites us to an inward journey; a place where we hear his still small voice and enter into his heart. Our God desires to communicate with us and show us his great love. He desires to be wanted.

Do you believe that?

Christina is a twenty-something girl in our town, who comes from a Christian family, goes to church regularly, and has attended Bible school. She says, "God doesn't talk to me. He talked to a few people in the Bible, and he might talk to pastors, but he doesn't talk to most people, and he doesn't talk to me." Is that your experience? If so, it is my goal in this book to change your mind. God does talk to ordinary, everyday, normal Christians. And he will talk to you.

Stop for a moment and listen to God's heart as he speaks to his people Israel: "I am the one who brought them out of Egypt so I could live among them" (Ex. 29:46). They were to be his people, and he would be their God, and he would pour out his love and blessings on them.

This message of God is consistent throughout the Bible. In the New Testament Jesus told his followers: "Now you are my friends, since I have told you everything the Father told me" (John 15:15). Jesus' words were genuine. He was inviting his followers to enter into communication and community with him.

Following Christ's resurrection, two disciples were engaged in a deep conversation with Christ as they walked the seven miles from Jerusalem to the village of Emmaus. They had not been aware that they were indeed walking with Jesus. But when he left their side, they suddenly realized that it had been the Messiah. They were changed! Why? Because no one is ever quite the same after having heard the voice of Christ. That is why we journal. We want to catch the message and the moment in writing!

In this book I want to engage you in at least three pursuits: to learn how to hear God's voice, to enter into conversation with him, and to record some of these conversations in your journal. I am fully aware that this work can only be done in our lives through the indwelling of the Holy Spirit. But I'm also aware that if we *don't* take time, we'll never *have* the time for the inner journey.

Clement of Alexandria testified that, "Prayer is keeping company with God." In other words, it is developing a conversational relationship with God. There are different ways to come at this insight; however, this discovery opened up to me through the practice of journaling. This journey is as exciting as the discovery. I invite you to let my story inspire you also to hunger after a friendship with God which is built on a two-way communication.

Introduction

SOME YEARS AGO I BEGAN JOURNALING. AS I LOOK BACK OVER THOSE times in which journaling was a part of my life, I see they were often written during times of stress and uncertainty. What is particularly gratifying is to see how insights gleaned in those times became so central to life and ministry. My regret is that they were not consistently entered.

As Vern points out, journaling is a marvelous way to learn to hear God's voice. While we learn to hear him speak in so many ways, the discipline of keeping a journal helps us engage with a medium that brings together the study of the Word, devotional prayer, and the tuning of one's ear to hear God speak.

Surely the exercise is learning to listen. Hearing God is tough. In contrast to the noise and distractions in our contemporary world, God's voice is gentle, not overpowering other noises and voices. If we are to hear, we have to learn to listen and do it intentionally.

As you read this most helpful book, you will be reminded that God speaks in many ways. For me, in times I needed his leading in ministry, I've often heard his voice out of biblical stories. Let me use an example.

I had spent a number of years in a national Canadian ministry, representing the evangelical community to government and media, making sense of what the Spirit was saying as to our biblical engagement with our surrounding culture.

One night I received a call from a school—over a hundred years old with both an undergraduate and a graduate program in Bible and theology—asking if I would help as they were in major difficulty. After discussing it with my executive I agreed to help for a few months as a volunteer. The few months stretched into a year. The new board then asked if I would come as president. Nothing could have been further from my interest or sense of calling.

As Lily and I considered the request, I recalled a message by pastor Jack Hayford titled "Abraham's Unalterable Need for Altars." His thesis was this: as Abraham walked in faith, from time to time he would build an altar as a witness to lessons he was learning. In time, and especially when instructed to sacrifice Isaac's life, he looked back over the altars he had built, using them to guide him in this most difficult of decisions.

Lily and I reflected on this story. I asked, "What are the vocational altars I've built?"

As Lily recounted the "altars" I had built through the various ministries I had led, I "heard" the Spirit saying, "You've built and repaired ministries in the past, now I have another major job for you."

The Lord knew I needed that moment of hearing. For later, as I worked my way along the path of reconstructing the schools—Tyndale University College & Seminary—there were days in which the downright doggedness of this task led me to wishing I was in the former ministry I had so dearly loved. This takes us full circle back to the importance this book can be to you.

On that day I journaled, recording the moment, the insight, the message. Often over the intervening years I would look for those pages and reread what I had heard that day, years ago. Thank goodness I had entered that moment in my journal, for in making that entry, it has stayed fresh in my memory as a moment in which the Lord so faithfully led. The logic of course is, given he led me that day he will do the same today and tomorrow.

Take Vern's counsel on learning to listen seriously. It will sharpen your listening skills, and that in turn will transform your walk. It will deepen your understanding of the Spirit's work. It will help clarify your thinking in times of confusion. It will help you build a daily discipline to hear the voice of the Spirit, so that from the Word and your dialogue of prayer you will be led and empowered in service.

If I can persuade you of anything it is this: Don't end up at the end of your life and ministry without having had the enormous learning experience that comes from journaling, and without having the rich material that will record the "Acts of God" in your life.

Brian C Stiller
President
Tyndale University College & Seminary

1

An Invitation to Listening to God

"My sheep recognize my voice; I know them, and they follow me."
—John 10:27 MSG

When the journal opens, so does the ear of my heart. If God is going to
speak, I am ready to listen.
—Gordon MacDonald[1]

"I'LL NEVER FORGET THE SUMMER I ATTENDED A LADIES BIBLE STUDY," writes Terry, "and learned how to prayer journal. I was at the end of my rope with my unsaved husband, and seriously contemplating divorce. I had tried everything to bring my husband to the Lord … dragging him to church, praying for him, and leaving hints around the house … even fridge magnets that said 'Jesus loves you.' Nothing worked, and we were in trouble in every way. Then God stopped me cold in the Bible study when I read 1 Peter 3:1. I could not for the life of myself figure out how God was going to save my husband if I didn't help along. How could I "not say a word" and my husband would actually be won to the Lord by my behavior? Anyway, I figured I didn't have much to lose so at this point, I obeyed and kept my mouth shut from then on. It was July when my husband gave his life to Christ through the testimony of his boss at work. Go figure!" Journaling helped Terry process her frustration and faith before the Lord. A miracle happened. Both her and her husband's lives changed.

The Lord delights in affirming his work in us. Every once in a while he gives us an insight into what he's doing behind the scenes. For example, several months ago my wife, Carol, and I were enjoying a meal at a restaurant out of town. After we had finished dinner and paid the check, we walked over to our car and were about to leave the premises. Then, somewhat to our surprise, we noticed a man coming toward us, waving his hand and giving us a smile of recognition. I opened the car window, and he introduced himself as a person who had sat through a seminar on listening to God and journaling I had taught about eight years earlier. In the relatively brief conversation we had, he passionately related how the discipline of journaling had brought him into a new intimate knowledge of his Lord. He continued by saying, "Next to receiving Christ as my Savior, journaling has been one of the most important decisions I have made in my Christian life." When he saw me, he realized he wanted to say thank you for being introduced to the discipline of journaling. Similar stories in varied forms can be told by other individuals who have begun and continued this practice.

When I refer to journaling in a seminar or sermon, it usually draws immediate attention and evokes interesting questions. They often include inquiries such as, "What do you include in your journal?", "Who do you allow to access your journal?", "Does your wife read it?", and "How do you stick with it?" I will deal with some of these questions in later chapters.

A PERSONAL RECORD

I began journaling about twenty-five years ago. I soon realized that journaling was a personal record of my journey with God through the many and varied experiences of life. I also discovered that there is something about interacting and responding to Scripture, impressions, and visions, that, in writing them down, made them more memorable. I learned how to hear God's voice through the practice of journaling.

Jesus gives us words to reflect upon and to listen to carefully when he says, "My sheep recognize my *voice*; I *know* them, and they *follow* me" (John 10:27 MSG). Have you ever heard Jesus' *voice*—and kept a record of those times? Do you worship the Lord because he *knows* you and is totally acquainted with you? Have you ever kept a travelogue of your experience of *following* the Good Shepherd through the difficulties and the delights of life?

Charles Swindoll speaks about the intimacy he discovered with his Lord through keeping a record: "My journal became the anvil on which most of my private thoughts were hammered out."[2] There's something about writing out an experience, a confession, an anxiety, a prayer, or an expression of praise that helps everything become more specific, focused, and faith producing.

Gordon MacDonald writes about his journaling experience as follows: "Slowly, I began to realize that my journal was helping me to come to grips with an enormous part of my inner person that I had not been fully honest about."[3] This reminds me of the words of Jesus: "And you will know the truth, and the truth will set you free" (John 8:32).

HERE'S MY STORY

Many of the most significant beginnings in my life have come through the Lord's dropping a seed-thought into my mind and heart. This often comes through reading the Scriptures, enjoying a good book, or having a friend throw an offhand comment my way and later discovering that it was from the Lord.

The first significant reference to a journal that deeply impressed me was that of missionary Jim Elliot. At age 27 he died a martyr's death by the spear of an Auca Indian. In his journal, these words were inscribed: "He is no fool who gives what he cannot keep to gain that which he cannot lose." These words put meaning into his early violent death. In his journal, he had shaped his values and focused his life. He did all that God asked him to do. And because he kept a journal, we can be inspired through what God taught him.

Whenever we desire to undertake a new discipline or direction with the Lord that we know is of the Holy Spirit—for every good and godly desire does come from him—we need to recognize that implementing that discipline or direction still requires taking practical steps.

When I first began journaling it felt like taking a dive into a cool pool. It was refreshing, but also a brand new experience for me. I bought my first journal at a local stationery store. It was a hardback book with all blank pages. I sat down with pen in hand and wrote these first two short paragraphs as my first entry:

"I begin this journal because I sense this year will be a time of transitions for me and it is my desire to be fully conscious of what is happening to me.

Together with this, I covet a greater degree of personal discipline in my life, so God's grace will have ample opportunity to work through my life."

Next, I searched the Bible for an appropriate Scripture passage to use to begin this practice. I took these words from the Gospel of Luke: "Jesus grew in wisdom and stature, and in favor with God and men" (Luke 2:52 NIV). The observation I made was that as the Father had sent Jesus into the world, so he was sending me into that same world (John 20:21). So I began writing down areas in which I required growth in wisdom, stature, and favor with God and people. Once a month, I blocked off a number of hours to do this in the presence of the Lord. These proved to be rich times of praying, envisioning, and writing. My sometimes disconnected purposes and prayers went deeper into God's thoughts and words. I experienced times of confession, worship, and pure delight. It was good! Surprisingly, as I look back on that beginning, it wasn't as important how I journaled it as it was that I journaled. Yes, I had a learning curve.

THE NEXT STEP

Some years later, I heard Bill Hybels sharing at a leadership conference in San Diego. He spoke to us about his busy lifestyle and how he was caught in so much "doing" that he was losing out on the "being"—he was losing sight of what God wanted him to become. As the pastor of a growing church with eleven thousand attendees, he was often too busy to pray. The Lord led him to begin journaling. His story was very similar to mine. He visited a stationery store, bought a book, and became serious about keeping a record of his prayers, experiences, and insights before the Lord. In the book he later wrote about this experience, *Too Busy Not to Pray*, he wrote these passionate words: "Authentic Christians are persons who stand apart from others, even other Christians, as though listening to a different drummer. Their character seems deeper, their ideas fresher, their spirit softer, their courage greater, their leadership stronger, their concerns wider, their compassion more genuine, and their convictions more concrete. They're joyful in spite of difficult circumstances and show wisdom beyond their years."[4] He goes on to describe how authentic Christians are full of surprises because they're following a God who's always authentic with them.

I experienced a significant learning curve following this leadership conference. I recall spending time in my hotel room praying, promising, and desiring deeply to have a more intimate daily relationship with God. I must confess that it took significant discipline to carve out time for journaling each day. I learned, however, that the strength it brought to me spiritually was worth it all. Journaling became a journey.

The great thing about journaling is that God will personalize and help you understand the Scriptures as they pertain to you. Whether you are mainly confined to home, working in the marketplace, or a student attending school, thoughtfully reflecting on the Scriptures through journaling will make a huge difference in how you live and enjoy your walk with God.

ACTS

Later, inspired at a conference on prayer, I began using the acrostic ACTS to lead me through my Scripture reading and writing. This gave me a daily pattern to follow: Adoring God for who he is, Confessing my sins, Thanking him for his gifts, and bringing my Supplications (requests) before him.

Early on, by using this acrostic, I received two special blessings. First was my experience that adoring God for who he is made the confession of sins more real. Once I saw who God is and celebrated his compassion and love, it made the confessing easier and deeper.

Second, I found myself journaling through the books of the Bible that I would soon be using as sermon material in my pulpit ministry. As I did this, the Scriptures became more personal and opened up to me in new and dynamic ways. It was good to have the Spirit who inspired the Bible open the Scriptures to my heart. This gave me new joy and passion in my preaching.

GIVING THANKS

Through these daily times of journaling, I discovered a renewed sense of joy and thankfulness. God is continually showing me new ideas to incorporate into my journaling which make it enriching and enjoyable. Although there is no blueprint for exactly how to journal, let me share with you some of my own experiences. I recall sitting before the Lord one morning and wondering how I could give more thanks to him for all the goodness and mercy that he had shown towards me. I began doodling with the word "thanks" and came up with the following acrostic which helped me to express my thanks and live my gratitude in more practical ways.

T—Today

"This is the day the LORD has made. We will rejoice and be glad in it"
(Ps. 118:24).
I thanked God for his unique gift of this day that was before me. I saw it like a field of fresh fallen snow. It was my privilege to enjoy and celebrate it. So I thanked God for it.

H—Helper

"I think how much you have helped me; I sing for joy in the shadow of your protecting wings" (Ps. 63:7 MSG).
I thanked God specifically for a situation in which he had helped me the day before.

A—Answer

"I will call to you whenever I'm in trouble, and you will answer me"
(Ps. 86:7)
I thanked God for a prayer request he had answered the day before.

N—New

"I am about to do something new. See, I have already begun! Do you not see it?" (Isa. 43:19).

I thanked God for something new that I would experience that day. I simply went over my agenda for the day ahead of me and began thanking him for new people and experiences that would be mine.

K—Kind

"Love is … kind" (1 Cor. 13:4).
I thanked God for someone who had been kind to me in the past twenty-four hours. Often I would give that person a phone call or send an e-mail message to express my thanks for the kindness I had received.

S—Saying

"My sheep recognize my voice; I know them, and they follow me" (John 10:27 MSG).
I thanked God for something I had heard him speak into my life.

This little journaling exercise helped me to experience the reality of Paul's exhortation: "Be thankful in all circumstances, for this is God's will for you who belong to Christ Jesus" (1 Thess. 5:18). This little exercise of saying thanks to God is not intense or time consuming. As a matter of fact, it brought new zest to my time with the Lord. You may want to write a poem to the Lord one day, sing a song to the Lord another day, or draw a picture to glorify God at yet another time. There are many ways through which God communicates to you and you to him.

LISTENING

The place the Lord caught my attention was with the discipline of hearing God's voice—listening deliberately to hear what he was saying to me. I recall the first time I dared to write down something I sensed God was saying into my heart. It was an experience I entered into with some trepidation. I expected the Lord to scold me, or at minimum to warn me about all the things that endangered my life. However, I found the Lord saying things to me such as "I love you" and "I have good plans for your life." And then, God told me, "I have been waiting a long time to speak to you. Prayer has been a one-way street for you for too long. I want to speak into your life daily. I have important things to share with you." I was overwhelmed with the messages of love that I discovered in the Scriptures as God's voice was personalized in my life.

AN INVITATION

Journaling is not just for someone who has hours to spend at this discipline every day. It is something that each one of us can put into daily practice. We will never *have* time for devotions. We need to *take* time. As Bill Hybels says, "Any way you cut it, a key ingredient in authentic Christianity is time. Not left-over time, not throw-away time, but quality time. Time for contemplation, meditation, and reflection. Unhurried, uninterrupted time."[5]

A busy young executive summarizes his thoughts about journaling as follows: "Journaling has made my quiet times with the Lord more enjoyable. It has helped me to go to a deeper level of reflection on Scripture and to wait for the word that God wants to impress on me. Writing my thoughts and prayers has also solidified my communication with him. This has resulted in heightened anticipation of what God has for me today. This increased my faithfulness to my times with him." What this executive experienced is what all of us wish for in our time with the Lord. Journaling can be an important pathway to get there.

Today I have over fifty journal books standing on a shelf in my study. They are a record of many of the things I, together with my wife, children, and grandchildren, have experienced in life. The journals are not homework assignments to be handed in for correction. They are simply the thoughts and insights that God gave me as I experienced so much of his grace and ministry.

My goal is to encourage you to begin taking pen in hand and recording the thoughts that God gives you. The main thing is to wait on the Lord and begin recording your thoughts as you read the Scriptures and hear God's voice speaking your name.

Remember that everyone who hears God's voice is never the

same again. I invite you to discover the joy of developing a conversational relationship with God.

REFLECTION QUESTIONS

1. Have you ever kept a diary or a journal?

2. What were the difficulties you encountered in implementing your journaling discipline?

3. What steps will you take to overcome these barriers?

4. How could the use of the acrostic (THANKS) be of help to you as you express your gratefulness to God?

5. What are some other ideas you could incorporate into your journaling experience?

6. Read John 10:27: "My sheep recognize my voice; I know them, and they follow me" (MSG). Have you ever heard the Lord speak to you? When? What did he say to you?

2

Learning to Recognize God's Voice

After he has gathered his own flock, he walks ahead of them, *and*
they follow him because they know his voice.
—John 10:4

A sheep that has been with the shepherd for many years is better equipped
to hear the shepherd's voice.
—Charles Stanley[1]

IT IS AN AMAZING FACT THAT SHEEP AND OTHER DOMESTICATED ANIMALS
and pets unerringly recognize the voice of their master or mistress. The
Bible teaches that as surely as sheep recognize their shepherd's dis-
tinct voice, so also we have been given the capability to identify the
voice of Jesus, the Good Shepherd. Jesus said, "My sheep recognize
my voice; I know them, and they follow me" (John 10:27 MSG).

This truth was impressed on me during a visit that Carol and I
took to Israel several years ago. On a particular day, our schedule
called for a trip from Jerusalem to Jericho. About halfway into that
excursion, our guide stopped the bus near an old stone block building, which he identified as the Good Samaritan Inn. As we disem-
barked and listened to the information our guide gave us, we noted a
Bedouin shepherd was coming our way with a flock of sheep. The
shepherd approached me and said, "For one American dollar I'll show
you something special."

"All right then," I replied. I handed him his money and asked
him to "show us something special." Then, in his Arabic language, he
gave a crisp call. To our surprise, a sheep from the middle of the herd
pushed its way through the flock, stepped right up to the shepherd,

and nuzzled him. We all cheered. For another American dollar, he did the same thing with another sheep. The result was the same. The sheep responded immediately to the shepherd's call.

This little demonstration helped me to gain insight regarding Jesus' words, "My sheep recognize my voice ... and they follow me" (John 10:27 MSG). As surely as a sheep is able to discern the shepherd's voice, so also the Lord has given us the ability to hear and respond to his voice.

But what does God's voice sound like? Habakkuk, the prophet, learned to recognize the audible voice of God. The Scriptures record, "Then the LORD said to me, "Write my answer plainly on tablets" (Hab. 2:2). On the other hand, the prophet Elijah described God's voice as a still small voice or a "gentle whisper" (1 Kings 19:12). Then there was the child Samuel, who needed coaching from Eli to discern that the voice he heard was indeed the Lord's (1 Sam. 3:2–10).

Most of us, however, do not hear an audible voice speaking to us. Rather, God's inner voice comes to us as spontaneous thoughts, visions, feelings, promptings, or impressions. Allow me to illustrate. No doubt, as you have gone about your daily tasks, from time to time you have suddenly had an urge to pray for a specific person. We generally acknowledge that this is the Lord speaking to us, and we respond by praying. It was not an audible voice, but it was the Spirit directing our spontaneous thoughts. I have found that God speaks into our lives most often with this kind of inner voice. As I visit with fellow Christians, I soon discover that almost every one of them has had this kind of inner conversation with God. Sometimes we can hear God's voice by writing things out. It helps us to process the thoughts that are in our mind and in our heart.

When does God speak to me? And how do I know it is God speaking and not just some idea of my own? We would probably all agree that the Lord speaks to us during special times in our lives such as conversion, baptism, and marriage. But what about other times? I believe we need to be mentored in the art of listening to God's voice daily and taking the time to record the insights the Spirit gives us. In the rest of this chapter, I will give you seven ways to help you test whether an impression or inner voice is from the Lord.

Key 1: Is It Consistent with the Bible?

God's voice will never lead you to participate in any activity or relationship that is not consistent with his Word. Jesus made it clear: "Heaven and earth will disappear, but my words will never disappear" (Luke 21:33).

For example, there are too many believers who continue to feel guilty and condemned even though they have placed their faith in God. They sense an inner voice telling them that they are not good enough or that God is angry with them. If, however, we have confessed our sins, we have accepted Jesus' forgiveness, we are not involved in any disobedience, and we still feel guilty and condemned, then that voice is from the devil, not from God. We can be confident about that because the Bible tells us, "So now there is no condemnation for those who belong to Christ Jesus" (Rom. 8:1). In the book of Revelation, John clarifies that "The accuser of our brothers and sisters has been thrown down to earth—the one who accuses them before our God day and night" (Rev. 12:10). We need to understand how clearly the Scripture speaks to the issue of forgiveness and release from condemnation.

When you find yourself making a decision regarding finances, an occupation, a relationship, or some other significant issue, go to the Word of God and receive the Lord's guidelines for living. It is remarkable how a daily reading of the Scriptures will prepare you for the decisions you must make.

Remember, God never speaks against his own words. Be sure that the impressions and inner voice that you are receiving are from God. They should be consistent with his written Word.

Key 2: Does It Make Me More Like Jesus?

God's voice not only calls us to follow him but also transforms us into greater Christ-likeness. Paul puts it this way, "For God knew his people in advance, and he chose them to become like his Son" (Rom. 8:29).

Let me illustrate this in a family setting. During our years of ministry in San Jose, California, we often enjoyed the forty-mile drive south to Carmel by the sea. The beach was beautiful, and there were many places to explore. On one of these occasions, we found ourselves window shopping and enjoying the ambience of the city. Karla, our youngest child, was in the stroller. Our three sons, Murray, Bob, and Dave, were ahead of us, finding things that interested them. After a few minutes of this kind of activity, I lost sight of our three sons. I went from shop to shop to find them but had no luck. After some time, I began developing some anxiety about their whereabouts. Finally, as I entered one shop, the clerk by the door said to me, "Are you looking for three boys?"

"Why, yes," I replied with a measure of surprise.

"They are just around the corner looking at the toy display," she said with a twinkle in her eye.

Now she had me really curious, so I asked her, "How did you know I was looking for three sons?"

"It was easy," she replied. "They walk just like you do."

I found the three prodigals, but we left amazed at how easy it was for her to recognize the similarity between father and sons.

The application is obvious. When we hear God's voice and follow him, a genuine Christ-likeness is soon exhibited in our lives. It is a signal that Christ is truly at work in our lives. We are transformed more and more into the image of Christ. His voice leads us in that great transformation.

KEY 3: DOES IT CHALLENGE ME TO BECOME STRONGER IN FAITH?

The Bible reminds us that "we live by believing and not by seeing" (2 Cor. 5:7), that "faith comes from hearing, that is, hearing the Good News about Christ." (Rom. 10:17), and that only by faith can we please God (Heb. 11:6). Therefore, the Spirit is continually challenging us to step out in faith according to his promptings.

When God speaks to us, he invites us to trust him fully in the ministries he has tailor-made just for us. Just as Peter was invited to step out in faith when he saw Christ walking on the water (Matt. 14:25–32), so also we are prompted to test our trust in God. This big fisherman was moved from sight to faith by the Savior's invitation. Even so, you and I will find God calling us to live by faith on a daily basis. God's voice is always a call to faith and faith-fulness.

KEY 4: DOES MY CHURCH FAMILY CONFIRM IT?

We are not "Lone Ranger Christians." When we think we hear a strong word from the Lord, we should test it with mature Christians. Do the people in our circle of fellowship affirm what we believe the Lord is saying to us? Does it have the ring of truth so clearly that it can be affirmed by those who know us best?

On every occasion when Carol and I have made a major move in our ministry, we have called together people who know us well to help us discern God's will. There is a wonderful measure of peace that this brings. As a church, we are members of one body, and we truly need each other's insights to confirm what God is saying.

Centuries ago this discipline was already given. For example, St. Francis wisely directed his friend back into the fellowship of the church, saying, "but before you consent to inspiration in things which are of great importance, or that are out of the ordinary way, always consult your advisor."[2]

Another dimension to this principle is our relationships. Jesus declared, "If two of you agree here on earth concerning anything you ask, my Father in heaven will do it for you. For where two or three gather together as my followers, I am there among them" (Matt. 18:19–20).

A married couple exhibits great wisdom in decision making when they listen to the insights God has given each of them—because when two agree, then Christ promises to be a part of that circle of faith.

If, however, you are single, then it is critical for you to develop significant relationships with others in the Christian community with whom you can test out the promptings the Holy Spirit is giving you.

I have discovered that God often leads us to get advice from others, particularly from brothers and sisters who are mature in their faith. We do well to bring such people into our circle of council and confidence. The Bible says it this way: "Victory depends on having many advisers" (Prov. 24:6).

When you think you have a word from the Lord, it is important to test it out with a fellow believer. This could give you further insight and greater security in the direction you are taking.

KEY 5: DOES IT CALL FOR COURAGE?

When God speaks, he usually calls us to an act of courage. This can be anything from confessing a wrongdoing to trusting God with our resources. Repeatedly God calls us to acts of courage, because such acts honor our heavenly Father and he promises to be with us in doing them. (By the way, God does not argue with us or force us to do anything. He wants us to follow him as a response of love and faith in him.)

One of the most outstanding calls to courage in the Bible is that which was given to Joshua. His charge to defeat all the forces of evil in the Promised Land was daunting. What did God say to him? It is profound and instructive. God said, "This is my command—be strong and courageous! Do not be afraid or discouraged. For the LORD your God is with you wherever you go" (Josh. 1:9). The call to courage is connected with the promise of his presence. In the same way, when God challenges us to courage for a specific task, he will be there providing us with everything that is required. You will need courage to share your testimony, to be baptized, to go on a mission assignment, or to go through a serious time of illness. Courage begets courage as you hear God's voice.

Courage is also closely related to patience. Listen to what the psalmist says: "Wait patiently for the LORD. Be brave and courageous. Yes, wait patiently for the LORD" (Ps. 27:14). Courage includes the strength to wait for God's timing.

Courage is indeed a test for the authenticity of God's voice in your life.

KEY 6: DO I SENSE GOD'S PEACE?

When God speaks to us, his Spirit gives us the gift of peace and calmness in our spirit. The Bible gives us clear reassurance that if you bring your needs and anxieties to the Lord, "You will experience God's peace, which exceeds anything we can understand. His peace will guard your hearts and minds as you live in Christ Jesus" (Phil. 4:7).

When I was diagnosed as having Parkinson's disease several years ago, I found myself filled with anxiety. My body wasn't functioning normally, and this also impacted the way I felt and moved. One of my greatest joys in ministry was preaching, but now this became a chore for me. I also found myself having to make many adjustments to reorder my life to fit with the reality of what was happening in my body.

During this time I continued my journaling. I listened to God and asked for the peace which is more wonderful than the human mind can understand. I made a discovery that sometimes the peace that we receive is just enough for the next hour or the rest of the day. The discipline of journaling became an important way for me to have faith conversations with my God. He reminded me daily of his love and care. This enabled me to remind him of his call and his ownership of my life. The peace I discovered was not something I worked for, but rather it was a wonderful gift from God's heart. It was putting into practice the Bible's teaching to "Let the peace that comes from Christ rule in your hearts. For as members of one body you are called to live in peace. And always be thankful" (Col. 3:15). Literally, the phrase in this verse is, "Let the peace of Christ rule in your heart." As Christ rules in our hearts in the various experiences of life, he brings with him a peace that surpasses our understanding. It is part of hearing the voice of God.

Thomas Kelly says, "Over the margins of life comes a whisper, a faint call, a premonition of richer living which we know we are passing by. Strained by the very mad pace of our daily outer burdens, we are further strained by an inward uneasiness, because we have hints that there is a way of life vastly richer and deeper than all this hurried existence, a life of unhurried serenity and peace and power."[3]

KEY 7: DOES IT CALL FOR HUMILITY?

God is humble and speaks to us in messages that call for humility. Long ago King David declared: "He leads the humble in doing right, teaching them his way" (Ps. 25:9). Jesus invites us to come to him when we are stressed out and burdened down, because he has rest for our souls. For this reason, Jesus revealed himself to be "humble and gentle" (Matt. 11:28–30). This is how he communicates with us.

A. W. Tozer makes the observation that, "religion has accepted the monstrous heresy that noise, size, activity, and bluster make a man dear to God. But we may take heart. To the people caught in the tempest of the last great conflict, God says "Be still, and know that I am God" (Ps. 46:10). He continues, "Our strength and safety lie not in noise but in silence."[4] James says it this way: "God sets himself against the proud, but showers favor on the humble" (James 4:6). Paul confirms this with the statement, "your attitude should be the same that Christ Jesus had. Though he was God, he did not demand and cling to his rights as God. He made himself nothing; he took on a humble position of a slave and appeared in human form. And in human form he would humble himself even further by dying a criminal's death on the cross" (Phil. 2:5–8).

Yes, we hear the voice of God when we humble ourselves before him. It is at that point that the resistance in our hearts is broken down and we clearly hear what God has to say to us.

RECOGNIZING GOD'S VOICE

Learning to recognize God's voice is basic to our joy in following him. When you are faced with a difficult decision and wonder whether the messages you are hearing are from God, ask yourself: Is it consistent with the Bible? Does it make me more like Jesus? Does it challenge me to become stronger in my faith? Does my church family confirm it? Does it call for courage? Does it bring the gift of God's peace, and does it call for humility?

Most of us have been tutored in talking to God in prayer. We also should be encouraged to learn how to hear our Savior's voice personally. Samuel needed mentoring in understanding that God had spoken to him. Eli counseled him that he should say, "Yes, your servant is listening" (1 Sam. 3:10). I encourage you to make that your prayer as well.

LEARNING TO RECOGNIZE FALSE VOICES

The voice of Self. The voice of self can be recognized by its constant drive to be gratified. It is selfish and short-sighted. Jesus had to do battle with that same human voice of self when he was in the garden of Gethsemane, and he prayed, "Yet I want your will to be done, not mine" (Matt. 26:39). Our Savior was not filled with self-pity or rationalization. Rather he won the victory over self by depending fully on the power of God.

Our human heart, however, is deceitful and can be easily misled. The prophet Jeremiah put it this way, "The human heart is the most deceitful of all things, and desperately wicked. Who really knows how bad it is? But I, the Lord, search all hearts and examine secret motives" (Jer. 17:9–10). The only way we can recognize and identify the voice of self is to be filled with God's Word and controlled by the Holy Spirit. He will bring to our memory the truth of God's Word and will expose self for what it is. The Holy Spirit, "… will teach you everything and will remind you of everything I have told you" (John 14:26).

When self speaks, it is important to deal with its pull and power in behaving. Listen to what the Scriptures say: "The temptations in your life are no different from what others experience. And God is faithful. He will not allow the temptation to be more than you can stand. When you are tempted, he will show you a way out so that you can endure" (1 Cor. 10:13). That's good news. But we need to take the way of escape that God provides early on, or else we'll find self becoming more powerful in our life.

Peter, a disciple of Jesus, could not grasp the idea of his Savior's going to the cross. His self took upper hand and he shouted out, "This will never happen to you!" Jesus turned to Peter and said, "Get away from me, Satan! You are a dangerous trap to me. You are seeing things merely from a human point of view and not from God's" (Matt. 16:22–23).

Our old "self" is devious, cunning, and powerful. We can never bring it to heel on our own strength. We require the power of God and the presence of the Holy Spirit. It is important to learn how to recognize the voice of self immediately. Usually it's because it cries out for self-gratification or pity.

The voice of Satan. Satan's voice is cunning and deceitful as well. He can come like a roaring lion to frighten us or as an angel of light to accuse us.

Early on—in the Garden of Eden—Adam and Eve were confronted by this powerful foe. The tactics that Satan used are described in Genesis 3.

- He encountered Eve when she was alone. "Did God really say that you must not eat from any of the trees in the Garden?" (Gen. 3:1).
- He sowed seeds of doubt in God's Word. "You won't die!" the serpent hissed. "God knows that your eyes will be opened as soon as you eat it, and you will be just like God" (vv. 4–5).
- He gave bold promises. "You will become just like God" (vv. 4–5).
- He deceived Eve. "The woman was convinced. She saw that the tree was beautiful and its fruit looked delicious, and she wanted the wisdom it would give her. So she took some of the fruit and ate it." (v. 6).
- Both Adam and Eve ate. "Then she gave some to her husband, who was with her, and he ate it, too." (vv. 6–7).
- Both Adam and Eve recognized that they were naked. "At that moment their eyes were opened, and they suddenly felt shame at their nakedness. So they sewed fig leaves together to cover themselves" (v. 7).

The strategy that Satan used is still being employed today. He tries to speak to us when we are alone. He seeks to instill doubt in our minds. He makes promises that cannot be kept. And finally, he draws us into sin with its shaming consequences. Jesus said that "The thief comes only to steal and kill and destroy" (John 10:10 NIV).

Satan also tries to destroy us by speaking untruth about us. He tries to convince us that our sins are not forgiven, that we have very little value to God, that no one will ever see what we are doing and that Jesus doesn't care about the little things. The truth is, Satan speaks lies into our life so that we will fall, even as Adam and Eve fell.

Satan is also a cunning user of the Scripture. When our Savior was tempted for forty days and nights in the wilderness, Satan used Scriptures out of context to try to confuse and bring Jesus to fall. Christ, however, knew the Scriptures well enough to stymie Satan. In the same way, if we learn the Scriptures and are filled with the Spirit, we will realize at the moment of temptation that the Spirit is giving us the right Scriptures to use to combat him. Remember, God's voice will never contradict Scripture.

It is important for us to spend time daily in the Scriptures, for it is then that we tuck that Scripture away in our hearts and it can be used by the Holy Spirit when we are tempted. It is the Word of God that is powerful, a light and a revealer of truth. Satan is defeated. Let's not give in to his voice.

REFLECTION QUESTIONS

1. Read John 10:4: "After he has gathered his own flock, he walks ahead of them, and they follow him because they know his voice." How important is it to recognize and know God's voice?

2. What are some biblical examples of individuals who heard God's voice? What did they do about it?

3. How will most of us hear God's voice?

4. What are seven signals that help us discern whether a voice is from the Lord? Which ones are the most helpful to you?

5. Why is it that often only in retrospect do we clearly understand it was the Lord who spoke to us?

6. Do you agree with Charles Stanley, who noted, "A sheep who has been with a shepherd for many years is better equipped to hear the shepherd's voice"?

3

Primary Ways God Speaks to Us
(As Related to Journaling)

"Call to me and I will answer you and tell you great and unsearchable things you do not know."
—Jeremiah 33:3 NIV

Prayer catapults us onto the frontier of the spiritual life. It is original research in unexplored territory.
—Richard Foster[1]

JOURNALING CAN HELP US WORK THROUGH ISSUES THAT WE ARE dealing with. It's also a wonderful discipline that leads us to an active relationship with the Lord. Journaling leads us to a point of communicating with the God of the universe! Imagine that!

GOD'S OPEN DOOR

God created us for fellowship. We were made to have an intimate relationship with him, and it is through prayer that this relationship is matured and shaped. As believers in Christ, we have direct access to speak to God. In any circumstance, crisis, or challenge, we are invited to "come boldly to the throne of our gracious God. There we will receive his mercy, and we will find grace to help us when we need it most" (Heb. 4:16).

Oswald Chambers makes the observation that "Jesus never mentioned unanswered prayer. He had boundless certainty that prayer is always answered."[2] David, the king, shouts the same encouragement our way when he says, "May the LORD answer all your prayers" (Ps. 20:5).

If God promises to answer all our prayers, what do we say when there is no answer that we can perceive? I have struggled with this when I have prayed and the heavens have seemed as impenetrable as brass. I've also counseled many people who have been confused by this seeming silence on the part of God. Has this been your experience too?

The apostle John helps us work through this issue. By the Spirit, he was led to write, "And we can be confident that he will listen to us whenever we ask him for anything in line with his will. And if we know he is listening when we make our requests, we can be sure that he will give us what we ask for" (1 John 5:14–15 NIV).

Note the phrase "according to his will." Praying is an act of faith that includes discovering more of God's desire for us. We will have what we ask for *if it is according to God's will*. As we earnestly pray and seek his face, we will understand more of his passion and path for us.

Journaling can help us work through these issues. On many occasions I have written down a prayer and meditated on it for days, sometimes weeks. During this time of waiting, God spoke to me in many ways. But most often he either gave an answer or peace regarding the issue.

A HELPFUL TEMPLATE

Bill Hybels shares a very helpful little template to give us a measure of understanding in the matter of answered prayer:

- ❑ If the request is wrong, God says "No."
- ❑ If the timing is wrong, God says "Wait."
- ❑ If you are wrong, God says "Grow."
- ❑ If the request is right, the timing is right, and you are right, God says "Go."[3]

Let's take a closer look at each one of these statements. First, if the request is wrong, God says no. As a parent, I've had to learn how to teach my children the meaning of the term no! This protected them from many dangers and also gave them a sense of right and wrong.

Recently I was helping to paint my eighteen-month-old grandson's room. Riley had a high interest in what I was doing and peeked into the room on several occasions. I warned him with a stern no when he went for the paint tools and freshly painted wall. It was all so tempting for him. After completing the job, I cleaned up the room and left for home. Karla, his mother, was keeping an eye on him while she was doing some ironing. Suddenly she sensed that everything was too quiet in the house. Sure enough, she discovered her son had just finished rolling paint on the carpet, on the wall, and on himself. It was quite a sight! The no had to be reinforced again for Riley.

The Lord also says no to some of our requests, some of the things we ask for in prayer. The Lord loves us far too much to give us a yes to all of our desires. Our heavenly Father reminds us, "My ways are far beyond anything you could imagine. For just as the heavens are higher than the earth, so are my ways higher than your ways and my thoughts higher than your thoughts" (Isa. 55:8–9). We need to remind ourselves again and again that God has a purpose and design for our lives. When we are not in line with his thinking, he says a gracious and firm no to us!

At other times, God says wait because the timing is wrong. David was God's anointed to be the next king of Israel. This was clearly communicated to him by the prophet Samuel (1 Sam. 16:13). Shortly after this, however, a price was put on his head by the jealous King Saul, and he had to flee for his life. An occasion arose in this chase when David could have killed his arch foe, Saul. His own men urged him on by saying, "This is the day God was talking about when he said, 'I'll put your enemy into your hands. You can do whatever you want with him'" (1 Sam. 24:4). Here his own men seemed to be quoting a word of prophecy to justify killing King Saul. The circumstances seemed to be leaning in that direction. But David knew the timing was wrong, and the Lord said wait in response to this seemingly perfect opportunity for David to enter into his destiny. God loves us too much to say yes to all our requests. As a loving Father, he says wait to requests that are inappropriate or are not well timed.

There are also occasions when God says we are wrong, and he transforms our wrong request into an occasion for us to grow. Jesus had such an experience with his passionate disciples James and John. During one of their ministry tours, they were sent ahead by Jesus to find night quarters and ministry opportunities in a Samaritan town. The villagers, however, did not permit them to enter. The affronted disciples asked Jesus, "Should we call down fire from heaven to burn them up?" (Luke 9:54). They were wrong in their request. Jesus not only sternly rebuked them but also made this an occasion for them to grow. The Master sent them on to another village that received them. Among other things, Jesus taught his disciples to grow in their understanding of his patience and grace for stiff-necked people.

Finally, if the request is right, the timing is right, and you are right, God says go! This is where God, by his Spirit, does amazing miracles. He loves to answer such prayers.

The burgeoning church at Antioch experienced an explosive time of powerful prayer and intercession. While they were worshipping, fasting, and praying, the Holy Spirit spoke to them and said, "Dedicate Barnabas and Saul for the special work to which I have called them." After more fasting and praying, "the men laid their hands on them and sent them on their way" (Acts 13:2–3). This resulted in the Gospel being heard and responded to throughout the gentile world. The request was right—the gospel was designed to impact the whole world. The timing was right—the spiritually bankrupt Roman world was hungry for the Good News. Also, the church was right—they heard and obeyed the Spirit's promptings.

HEARING GOD'S VOICE

Keeping a record of what God says to you helps you to write your life story, and communicate God's leadings more specifically. Let me give you a current illustration. Kevin and Erin Peters serve as missionaries in Madagascar. Kevin is a helicopter mechanic. His responsibility is to keep these flying machines in good repair so that the missionaries and local Christians can reach the remote areas of the island with the Gospel. The Peters, however, sensed the Lord's calling them to get more directly involved in reaching people for Christ. They heard the

Spirit's prompting them to get involved in a project that would take them out of their city residence and into the frontier of mission work.

For two years they prayed about this passion, talked with friends, and listened for what the Lord would say to them. They observed that the many villages scattered in the remote northwestern part of the island had next to no missionary activity in them. The area was almost inaccessible by normal means of transportation, and danger lurked from armed cattle thieves who roamed this uncharted territory. The Lord began prompting them to reach into this difficult region.

The Peters shared their vision with other missionaries, but they all seemed to be too busy to add this to their ministry. So Kevin and Erin continued with their strategy of praying and listening. It was then that they became aware that some people from Canada were looking for a short-term mission opportunity to carry medical supplies to exactly this part of Madagascar. Kevin and Erin sensed the Lord was leading them to organize this mission.

The Peters were counseled to find a Christian Malagasy medical doctor who would be willing to live in the area for at least one year. It did not take long for them to find such a doctor. He met all of the qualifications and was excited to take the assignment. The funding was taken care of by interested persons. A Campus Crusade for Christ team committed themselves to translate various portions of the Scriptures and The JESUS Film into the local dialect. The Peters were able to help in the showing of The JESUS Film. The Lord not only gave them the vision but also in unique ways communicated the path they should follow to make the dream a reality. As we in their home church heard their story, not only were we filled with thanksgiving, but we were also deeply moved by the realization that the Lord had prompted them every step of the way.[4]

PRAYER IS A TWO-WAY CONVERSATION

God made us to have the kind of communication with him that runs both ways. After God created Adam and Eve, he walked in the garden in the cool evening with them (Gen. 3:8). They enjoyed a two-way conversation with their Creator. It was a dialogue.

Then there was Enoch, who "walked in close fellowship with God. Then one day he disappeared, because God took him" (Gen. 5:24). He and God enjoyed fellowship so much that Enoch bypassed the step of dying before he entered God's presence. Surely, they enjoyed an intimate life of communication with one another.

It is fascinating to read in the Scriptures that Moses experienced God in such a way that "the LORD would speak to Moses face to face, as one speaks to a friend" (Ex. 33:11). We, too, are called God's friends: "I no longer call you servants, because a master doesn't confide in his servants. Now you are my friends, since I have told you everything the Father told me" (John 15:15).

Do you believe God still speaks to us today? There are those who believe that God has given us the Scriptures, and that he has already said everything he has to say. On the other hand, there are those who seem to believe that what they perceive to be God's Word to them overrides the written Bible. Often these individuals are driven by strong emotions.

Does God take an interest in the daily stuff of our lives? Is he too busy to get involved in the details of our decisions? Does he communicate and show his love to us individually and as a community?

Henry Blackaby gives us this good word of insight: "When God speaks, he does not give us new *revelation* about himself that contradicts what he has already revealed in Scripture. Rather, God speaks to give *application* of his Word to the specific circumstances of life."[5]

In other words, we are not writing an addition to the Bible when we hear God's voice; rather, when God speaks, he is applying to our lives what he has already revealed in the Bible. So your journaling becomes a wonderful connection between the written Word of God and the applied Word of God in your life.

LEARNING TO LISTEN TO GOD

We are familiar with the truth that we are invited to speak to God. Talking to God is almost a universal practice. But listening to God and hearing his voice is not nearly as commonly practiced. In all likelihood, most of us have not been mentored in hearing God's voice.

Peter Wagner writes, "Learning to hear the voice of God was a long process for me because it was such a radical departure from my past."[6] The key question is not; "Does God speak to us?" but rather, "Are we listening to his voice?" Dan is a mature Christian who began journaling several months ago. He writes, "Journaling has made my quiet time with the Lord more enjoyable. It has helped me go to a deeper level of reflection on Scripture and wait for the word that God wants to impress on me. Writing my thoughts and prayers has also solidified my communication with him. This has resulted in a heightened anticipation of what God has for me today, which has increased my faithfulness in my times with him."

In the next few chapters I will describe eight primary ways in which God speaks to us. Your journal will become a rich repository as you keep a record of God's words and visions to you.

REFLECTION QUESTIONS

1. Do you agree with the statement: "Jesus had boundless certainty that prayer is always answered"?

2. Does God answer all your prayers? How do you know?

3. Have you ever been able to process or "hear God's voice" through writing out your thoughts? Are you willing to try?

4. Do you truly believe that God will speak to you and give you his directions as he did with Kevin and Erin Peters?

5. Read Jeremiah 33:3: "Call to me and I will answer you and tell you great and unsearchable things you do not know" (NIV). What does this Scripture mean?

6. How can journaling your prayers encourage you in your prayer life?

4

God Speaks to Us through the Bible

Every part of Scripture is God-breathed and useful one way or another—showing us truth, exposing our rebellion, correcting our mistakes, training us to live God's way.
—2 Timothy 3:16 (MSG)

If you would follow on to know the Lord, come at once to the open Bible expecting it to speak to you. Do not come with the notion that it is a thing which you may push around at your convenience. It is more than a thing, it is a voice, a word, the very Word of the living God.
—A. W. Tozer[1]

THE BIBLE IS GOD SPEAKING

FAE BEGAN JOURNALING THROUGH THE SCRIPTURES, AND EARLY ON discerned God's voice speaking to her. The Word of God became clear to her as she read Ephesians 1:5, "His unchanging plan has always been to adopt me into his own family by bringing me to himself through Jesus Christ! And this gave him great pleasure." She writes, "I learned that because God loves me, I could love me too. Now I make my devotional and journaling time a priority. I'm amazed at the changes happening in my life." So, you see that as you practice your journaling, you will discover that God's voice is most clearly heard when you read the Bible. In the most primary sense, the Bible is simply God's speaking. So for us the important thing is learning how to listen.

It is not a coincidence that the Bible is referred to as the Word of

God. The Bible is God's primary way to speak with us today. In the Bible we have God's full revelation to us in written form. An old-time preacher once said, "When you open the Bible, God opens his mouth."

As we read and meditate on the Scriptures, an amazing process occurs: "God peels back our protective layers of hypocrisy until we see what he sees."[2] At that point God begins to have the opportunity to speak into our lives. It is through such prayerful reading of the Scriptures, actively listening for God's voice as you read, that you will discover verses and phrases that will simply "jump out at you." It is almost as if the Spirit uses a highlighter to underscore a message you need to hear at that moment or (as you may discover) a message you will need for a challenge that will come your way later in the day.

THE BREAD OF LIFE

"The Bible addresses every emotion, human relationship dynamic, problem of the heart, aspect of the psyche, temptation of desire, heartache or joy, or issue of faith, love, or hope."[3] The Bible speaks to every issue of life. That is why we need to read it, meditate on it, obey it, and nurture our life on it as the very bread from heaven (John 6:34).

Just as our body requires nourishing meals every day in order to function at its optimum, so also does our spiritual life require the bread of life in order to maintain a vigorous walk with God. A helpful illustration of this comes our way from the experience Israel had when they were led through the wilderness by Moses. They received the gift of manna from God as described in the Scriptures: "The people gathered the food morning by morning, each family according to its need. And as the sun became hot, the flakes they had not picked up melted and disappeared" (Ex. 16:21). Every day the manna had to be gathered. They could not collect and store it for a number of days. It had to be their daily experience. (The only exception was that they could gather a double portion on Friday so they would not have to work on the Sabbath.)

Note also that the morning is the time to gather the manna and to spend unhurried fellowship with the Lord. David also exhorts us to have this "early morning" experience with God: "In the morning, O LORD, you hear my voice; in the morning I lay my requests before you and wait in expectation" (Ps. 5:3 NIV).

Recently a renowned minister shared some research he had done regarding the devotional life of the average evangelical Christian. It was his contention that only twenty percent of believers have a daily time with the Lord, reading and studying his Word. Is it any wonder that there is a lack of spiritual strength, wisdom, and discernment in the way believers live? Regardless of the time of day, it is necessary to find a time that works for you!

Think of it this way: If the only spiritual meal you have is the Sunday sermon, from where will your spiritual strength come? That is like trying to get by on a little spiritual snack here and there but missing the solid nourishing meals that God has provided for us each day.

GOD'S WORD IS PERSONAL

The Word of God is personal. Hearing God's voice through Scripture is only for those who are ready to listen. Yet remarkable things happen when we listen for and hear God's voice.

Henry and Richard Blackaby tell this story. "The city of London was frozen to a halt by a hostile blizzard. It was January 6, 1850—a Sunday morning. That alleviated the necessity for many people to brave the elements for work. Few attempted the trek to church. One young man, however, felt powerfully compelled to find a house of worship. At his mother's suggestion, the fifteen-year-old set out for the church in Colchester. He was unsuccessful; the storm was too fierce. He stumbled upon the Artillery Street Primitive Methodist Church. Only a handful of hardy members—fifteen, to be exact—had successfully forged their way there. The pastor had been unable to navigate the streets. When it became apparent this group would constitute the congregation, a thin angular man agreed to share a few words from the pulpit. He took as his text Isaiah 45:22 (KJV): "Look unto me, and be ye saved, all the ends of the earth." The unlettered layman stumbled over the passage for several minutes. Then he focused his gaze on the troubled teenager trying to sit inconspicuously in the balcony. Pointing his long, bony finger at the startled boy, he shouted, 'Young man, you're in trouble! Look to Jesus Christ! Look! Look! Look!' Young Charles Spurgeon did turn to Christ in that unexpected moment, and from that cumbrous message emerged a convert who would become one of the greatest preachers in the modern era. God speaks when he chooses. Storms don't stop him. Neither do novice speakers. The Holy Spirit is not restricted to polished outreach programs and silver-tongued orators. God had something to say to a British teenager that day, and that message, directly out of God's Word, was hand delivered to Charles Spurgeon."[4]

The Word of God speaks powerfully when read personally or heard publicly. When you read the Word of God, you hear the voice of God. Reading the Bible is God's invitation to us to intimately hear his voice and apply it to our lives. Journaling this conversation can be a great help in thinking through the issues God presents to you.

FORMATIONAL READING

Reading the Scriptures to hear God's voice is a wonderful discipline to learn. Robert Mulholland helps us to understand that there are basically two ways that we can read the Scriptures. First, we can read them to get information. This is a valid way of reading the Bible. But he explains that there is also a way to read it for transformation. This way of reading is a way of listening, of being present in the text. Look at the comparison below.[5]

INFORMATIONAL READING	FORMATION READING
We cover as much as possible as quickly as possible.	We are not concerned with amount read, with "getting this book done." We are willing to wait before the text.
We move from a to b to c, in linear direction over the face of the text.	We read in depth, allowing the passage to open out to us in its multiple layers of meaning.
We exercise control through analysis, passing judgment, organizing the content. We decide what is important, and how it is to be lined up. The text is the object over which we have control.	We are servants and become mastered by God who speaks through the Word. Here we experience an open receptivity, a willingness for creation and formation of the new person in Christ.

Informational Reading	Formation Reading
We seek information to enhance our ability to function so as to change the world to our parameters.	The content serves to change the quality of our being. We become open to discover God's Reality—the kingdom of God, the "mind of Christ."
We come with a problem-solving mentality and read to find something that will work for us, fix what we are uncomfortable with.	We are receptive to the probing of the Holy Spirit, taking time to listen, to be open to mystery.
We keep the text at a distance.	We are receptive to the Holy Spirit's shining the truth of God in the inner space within us—our heart space.
This involves human effort, analysis.	We receive Spirit, gift, revelation.
Here we want to know.	Here we become known.

We need both kinds of reading. But we also must realize that the Scriptures can only be understood through the same Holy Spirit who gave them to us in the first place by his inspiration. Therefore, this living Word of God must be received by us as God's speaking into our lives.

Peter encourages us this way: "We were also given absolutely terrific promises to pass on to you—your tickets to participation in the life of God after you turned your back on a world corrupted by lust" (2 Peter 1:2–3 MSG).

The primary way in which God speaks to us is through the Scriptures. This is the plumb line for every other means God uses to speak to us. It is as we let our hearts be filled with God's Word that God will open our spirit's ears to hear him and our eyes to see him through other ways as well.

REFLECTION QUESTIONS

1. Read 2 Timothy 3:16 (MSG): "Every part of Scripture is God-breathed and useful one way or another—showing us truth, exposing our rebellion, correcting our mistakes, training us to live God's way." What is the basic message of this verse? How does this impact us?

2. What is the similarity between manna in the experience of the Israelites and reading the Scriptures in the experience of a New Testament Christian? How does this impact our life with God?

3. When did you have the most consistent personal devotional time with the Lord (what time of day works best for you)? How did this make a difference in your life?

4. What are the differences between reading the Scriptures "informationally" and "formationally"?

5. What helps you to recognize God's voice as you read the Bible?

6. Why is the Bible foundational to hearing God's voice?

7. How does journaling impact your use of the Bible for hearing God's voice?

5

God Speaks to Us through Impressions of the Holy Spirit

"The Holy Spirit—he will teach you everything and will remind you of everything I myself have told you."
—John 14:26

I make it my business to persevere in his Holy presence, wherein I keep myself by a simple attention and general fond regard to God, which I may call an actual presence of God; or, to speak better, an habitual, silent, and secret conversation of the soul with God; which often causes me joys and raptures inwardly, and sometimes also outwardly, so great that I am forced to use means to moderate them and prevent their appearance to others.
—Brother Lawrence[1]

You ARE NOT ON THIS JOURNEY ALONE! WHENEVER YOU OPEN GOD'S Word—it is living. The Holy Spirit is your teacher. Invite him to communicate with you as you journal.

It is not possible to enter God's family unless our Father himself makes the invitation. Jesus put it this way: "For no one can come to me unless the Father who sent me draws them to me" (John 6:44). And how does the Father communicate this invitation? The Holy Spirit was sent by the Father to convince us of everything that Jesus said, including "His great and precious promises" (2 Peter 1:4).

In his model prayer, Jesus teaches us to pray as follows: "And don't let us yield to temptation, but rescue us from the evil one"

(Matt. 6:13). As our divine Helper, the Holy Spirit speaks to our inner person with a no when we're in danger of yielding to Satan's temptations. The Spirit also delights in speaking a yes to those things that are good and bring glory to the Father. We can never ask the Spirit too often "Should I do this?" or "Should I not do that?" As we are encouraged to pray without ceasing (1 Thess. 5:17 KJV), so also we can be in conversation with the Holy Spirit without ceasing. Paul puts it this way: "Let the Holy Spirit fill and control you" (Eph. 5:18). The original Greek, in which the New Testament was written, uses the present continued tense here, giving the sense, "Let the Holy Spirit be always filling and controlling you."

I have discovered that the Holy Spirit communicates with me very personally. He is the divine Helper whom Jesus had sent to shepherd us in our daily life.

REMINDERS

The Holy Spirit is a divine reminder. He "will remind you of everything I myself have told you" (John 14:26).

When our four children were in their elementary school years, we were living in California, where spring comes early and the sun shines hot. Our table conversation was always interesting, and various issues usually surfaced during that time. One day the conversation turned to an interesting request.

"We need a swimming pool," I was informed by our active children. It didn't take too much convincing to persuade me that it was hot and that this would be a fun piece of recreational equipment to have in our backyard. Carol and I agreed that this was a good project, but we didn't have the cash to buy an $800 portable pool for our backyard enjoyment. I suggested that we make it a prayer request and see how the Lord would provide. I'm not so sure how impressed my children were with this strategy, but we did pray and were waiting to see what the Lord would do. So, for the next week or more, it was a matter of daily prayer that God would provide a swimming pool.

The weather, however, turned hotter, and there wasn't much splashing in the backyard. Finally I felt that I needed to help God out by purchasing a pool with my credit card. After all, what are credit cards for? So I picked up my wallet, grabbed my car keys, and took with me a brochure advertising a sale on swimming pools.

On the way to the car, the Holy Spirit stopped me. That still small voice was speaking to me. Forcefully he reminded me of the prayers we had spoken. The message was: "Vern, don't do it!" I hesitated, was convicted, and went back into the house. It wasn't very long before I found myself kneeling at one of my children's beds and praying for a miracle. By this time, the Spirit had convinced me that I was going about it the wrong way. So I reaffirmed my faith in God's prayer-answering power and got to my feet with a renewed quiet confidence.

It was no more than an hour and a half later that my neighbor, Walter England, a realtor, was at the front door asking for me. He greeted me with a whimsical smile and said, "Vern, I just sold a house down the road, and it has a portable eighteen-foot-diameter swimming pool in the yard. Might you be interested in it?

Like a true Mennonite, my first question was, "How much does he want for it?"

Walter replied, "It's free. The buyers just want it removed from their yard."

I was overwhelmed. I couldn't help but tell the realtor how he was an answer to a specific prayer. At the dinner table that evening, there was a lot of excitement. We talked about putting up the pool and having summer fun. The highlight, though, was reminding ourselves of the fact that God answers prayer. The Lord not only gave us a pool, but also protected us from unnecessary debt.

SCRIPTURE

The Holy Spirit speaks to us through reading the Scriptures and reminds us of the truths we have read there as we live out our daily lives. Our response to him is important. Journaling through the Scriptures, listening to our hearts, and responding to his voice are significant.

EVANGELISM

All areas of our lives are affected by our deepening relationship with him. In a special way the Holy Spirit also prepares us and guides us in introducing people to Jesus. The solid promise of Christ to us is: "When the Holy Spirit has come upon you, you will receive power and will tell people about me everywhere" (Acts 1:8).

At times, the Spirit may prompt us to do something as simple as giving someone a cup of cold water in his name. At other times, we may have an experience such as Philip had when the Holy Spirit commanded him to "Go over and walk along beside the carriage" (Acts 8:29). Philip obeyed the voice of the Spirit and found an Ethiopian whom the Spirit had prepared to listen to the Good News about Jesus. Today we experience the work of the Holy Spirit in a similar way. The Spirit prepares both the receiver and the communicator of the Gospel. As a matter of fact, we can rest assured that God will give us divine appointments every day as we walk according to his promptings.

In your journaling time, you can ask God to make his divine appointments known to you! I personally have discovered, that when I make this request of the Spirit, very seldom is there a day where an opportunity doesn't come my way. It's even helpful to keep a record of the obvious appointments, and record the surprises that he's given you in your journal as well.

DECISIONS

The Holy Spirit gives us wisdom in our decision-making. Jesus promised to send us the Counselor, the Holy Spirit who "will teach you everything and will remind you of everything I have told you" (John 14:26). We need the Spirit's presence and voice in the innumerable decisions we are called on to make daily.

Recently I was reading a book authored by Steve Fry, a songwriter and theologian. He tells a rather interesting anecdote in his life: "One afternoon, while taking a breather from the rigors of ministry, I was feasting on a peanut butter sandwich and watching Fred Flintstone beat up on Barney Rubble. I suddenly became aware of God's presence in the family room. Sensing God's presence in times of prayer and worship was not unusual, but this encounter caught me quite off guard. Feeling the tug of the Spirit within, my first impulse was to quickly turn off the television, lay aside my precious peanut butter sandwich and get on my knees. But just as I was reaching for the knob, I felt the Lord clearly say to me in that still small voice, 'No, I want to watch the Flintstones with you.' I cannot quite describe the mix of bewilderment and delight that registered emotionally. The impression came so quickly that it froze me for a moment. Was I really hearing God say he enjoyed cartoons? But, it only took another moment or two before the truth hit me. God was telling me that he wanted to share all of life with me, even those parts that I might consider mundane or even frivolous."[2]

There are countless mundane decisions that come our way every day. How comforting and encouraging it is know that the Holy Spirit desires to be involved in making those decisions.

I kept a diary during my last two years of high school and the first two years of Bible college. When I page through that book I am surprised at how many times the Holy Spirit nudged me to have greater trust in him and to make my life count for God. In a very real way we begin to see the habits we have and the sum total of our habits is the total of our character.

PRAYER

The Holy Spirit also guides us in our prayers. I received the Lord into my life at age seven, with my mother's help. I vividly recall the Spirit drawing me to the Lord and entering my life as Savior. The very next thing my mother did was to teach me how to pray. She prompted me with simple sentences that I prayed after her. Soon I felt confident enough to put together my own prayers. But I'll never forget the important lesson that my mother taught me—she taught me how to pray. You may be a new believer. You may be intimidated by the "how or what" of prayer. But as simple as it was for me as a child, so it can be for you. God wants to hear our hearts. He is much more interested in our hearts than what words we use. The most elegant prayers I have heard are from children and new believers, because they are fresh and honest.

In a similar way, the Holy Spirit helps us when we pray: "And the Father who knows all hearts knows what the Spirit is saying, for the Spirit pleads for us believers in harmony with God's own will"

(Rom. 8:27). Very simply, as we pray about specific issues, we need to ask the Holy Spirit to prompt us as we pray. And if we do not know how to pray, we can be confident that he who reads our hearts will also bring a perfect prayer on our behalf before our heavenly Father. He will open our eyes to see more, our minds to understand more, and our hearts to believe more. Ask the Holy Spirit to teach you to pray. It will transform you. Then write down what the Holy Spirit is saying to you. It will help you to process what he is communicating to your heart.

ARE WE LISTENING?

The Holy Spirit speaks to us when we listen for him: We are invited to "be still, and know that I am God!" (Ps. 46:10). With all the voices that call us and the noises that surround us, we can crowd out the Spirit's words. I have found that the Spirit does not argue with me or force me to do his bidding. It is when I become quiet before the Lord that I become aware of his impressions.

It is the Holy Spirit who inspired Jeremiah to write these words to a hurting people: "If you look for me wholeheartedly, you will find me. I will be found by you" (Jer. 29:13–14).

Listening to the Holy Spirit opens our minds to the greatness of God and the need for our faith to grow. C. S. Lewis put it this way: "If we consider the unblushing promises of rewards and the staggering nature of the rewards promised in the Gospels, it would seem that our Lord finds our desires not too strong but too weak. We are half-hearted creatures, fooling about with drink and sex and ambition when infinite joy is offered us, like an ignorant child who wants to go on making mud pies in a slum because he cannot imagine what is meant by the offer of a holiday at sea. We are far too easily pleased."[3]

When the Spirit speaks to us clearly, it is an opportune time to record these insights in our journals. These entries will remind us of the words the Spirit prompted in us, but will also build our faith as we serve the Lord with greater authority and power.

REFLECTION QUESTIONS

1. Read John 14:26: "But when the Father sends the Advocate as my representative—that is, the Holy Spirit—he will teach you everything and will remind you of everything I have told you." What do you learn about the Holy Spirit in this verse? What does this mean for us practically?

2. Why did God give us the gift of the Holy Spirit? How important is his voice in our hearts?

3. Share an occasion from your life where you sensed the Spirit's prompting you to do something. How often did the Spirit need to speak to you before you realized it was his voice?

4. Who taught you to pray?

5. How does the Holy Spirit help us in our prayers?

6

God Speaks to Us through People

So faith comes from hearing, that is, hearing the Good News about Christ.
—Romans 10:17

I also learned to expect his speaking to come through me to others.
—Dallas Willard[1]

GOD USES HUMAN TONGUES TO COMMUNICATE HIS MESSAGE TO others. We Christians are equipped with the gift of the Holy Spirit to do this in power and clarity. At times, the messenger may share God's message in a formal teaching situation. On other occasions, however, the Holy Spirit may speak the Word of the Lord through us in spontaneous and surprising ways. If the truth were known, we would be surprised and affirmed by how often God actually speaks through us.

The story of Jacob and his sons illustrates how uniquely God's message can be delivered. Because Joseph, the son of Jacob's beloved wife, Rachel, was his father's favorite, his brothers were jealous of him. One day Jacob sent Joseph to visit his brothers and see how everything was going with them. The brothers apparently were some distance away, tending their flocks at Shechem. When Joseph got there, the brothers were not to be found. But he met a certain man in the field who asked him, "What are you looking for?" (Gen. 37:15). When Joseph told him that he was looking for his brothers, the man said, "They are no longer here. I heard your brothers say they were going to Dothan" (Gen. 37:17). So, eventually he was able to find his brothers, and they, in a fit of rage, sold him to a passing caravan as a slave. Joseph was taken to Egypt, where he was elevated to be Pharaoh's chief minister, guiding Egypt through a famine and becoming a Bible hero. Eventually his brothers came to Egypt for food and discovered the brother they had mistreated so badly.

But there is more to the story. Where did that certain man in the field come from? The Bible does not waste words. It is obvious that God used him to be a vital communication link to help Joseph find his brothers. The man was a minor character in the drama—but he was not superfluous. If Joseph had not encountered that man, the whole story would have ended differently. Pharaoh would never have had Joseph's advice, advice that made Egypt the only place in the Near East with abundant grain during the famine. Jacob's family would never have migrated to Egypt. The Israelite people would never have been enslaved. There would have been no Moses, no exodus, no Ten Commandments. The history of the world would have been radically different.

Did the man in the field even remember meeting the teenager who couldn't find his brothers? Did he recall being part of a five-sentence conversation? And if he did remember the conversation, could he possibly imagine that that brief communication would change history?

There's no question that God sends messages through us and to us. Yet many times we fail to fully recognize and appreciate the critical messages that God wants to send through us. The Lord has given each of us spiritual gifts, abilities, and experiences which perfectly match with the needs of individuals in our community. We not only are called to *bring* messages but to *be* a message from God to people.

The Holy Spirit has also gifted the church with spiritual leaders who speak and model the Word of God. We're reminded by Paul that the Lord is the one who gave these gifts to the church: "the apostles, the prophets, the evangelists, and the pastors and teachers. Their responsibility is to equip God's people to do his work and build up the church, the body of Christ" (Eph. 4:11–12). When a pastor teaches the Word of God in the power of the Spirit, God speaks through him. Whether the Bible is being taught from the pulpit of a large church, in a small group setting, or in a two-person mentoring relationship, there will usually be a surprise factor—that is, the Lord will speak into the very issues that the people are dealing with. God places his words and thoughts on the tongue of the communicator so that they become the message of God.

God also speaks through parents. Certainly, this does not mean parents are perfect. But the Scriptures exhort children to "listen, my child, to what your father teaches you. Don't neglect your mother's teaching. What you learn from them will crown you with grace and clothe you with honor" (Prov. 1:8–9). Children show wisdom by giving attention to their parents' instruction, for God places special insights into the parents' hearts and minds that are specifically designed to be shared with their families. Just as Eli taught Samuel to recognize God's voice, so parents do well to teach their children to do the same. Parents who are well schooled in the Word and filled with the Holy Spirit are better prepared to raise their children in the fear and nurture of the Lord.

God especially delights in sending messages of love, encouragement, and hope. A journal is an excellent place to record these insights and our gratitude for them.

For example, when I was in grade eleven attending a Christian high school, studying was not near the top of my priority list. Athletics, hanging out, and having fun were the agenda I was following. It was no surprise that my grades were marginal. The Lord chose to address this problem in my life in a unique way.

My high school teacher, Mr. Neufeld, also taught a mid-week Bible class for the boys. I can only recall one session and one lesson from all the times that I attended—but that one lesson was powerful. The subject was "Discovering God's will for your life." About halfway through the session, I found myself leaning forward as I heard Mr. Neufeld explain that God had a wonderful plan for each of our lives. The more he used Scripture to explain this concept, the greater my interest was piqued.

After the session, I approached my teacher and with great anticipation asked him what he thought God's will might be for my life. I will never forget his response. He crossed his arms over his chest, waited a while, looked me directly in the eye and said, "God's will for you, Vern, is to begin taking your studies seriously. The rest will be taken care of by the Lord in due time." This wasn't quite the answer I had looked for or anticipated. But his words were from God.

I recall being on my knees that night and asking the Lord to change my priorities so that I would take my studies seriously. The change took faith, commitment, and work, but, by God's grace, the turn was made. Having heard the voice of God through my teacher made me eager to hear his voice in the future.

God also speaks through individuals of faith even after they have died. The life of Abel gives us this insightful illustration: "God accepted Abel's offering to show that he was a righteous man. And although Abel is long dead, he still speaks to us because of his faith" (Heb. 11:4). So if you have a relative or friend of faith who has passed on, that person's life is still speaking to you. This is an encouragement for all of us.

I encourage you to anticipate God's speaking to you through people. This would be a good reason for you to take your journal with you to a church service. As you listen carefully and hear the Spirit's prompting, you'll be able to record thoughts and impressions that come through the one who is the speaker. Also, when you find insights and quotes in biographies or Christian books, you'll want to record them in your journal as well. Quite simply, God speaks through people.

We have learned in this section that God speaks to us through people. In a later part of this book, we will speak directly to the issue of testing the messages we hear in order to discern whether they are from God or not.

REFLECTION QUESTIONS

1. Read Romans 10:17: "So faith comes from hearing, that is, hearing the Good News about Christ." What happens when we hear God's thoughts through people? How is faith built?

2. Give a specific illustration in which the Lord used a person to bring a message to you. Did that person realize he or she was doing it? How did you know it was from the Lord?

3. In the story of Joseph, how important was the man who told him where his brothers were? (Gen. 37:15).

4. How and through whom does God speak to you in your church family? Give a specific example.

5. When is the last time you recognized God's voice through your pastor? A friend? Or through a family member?

7

God Speaks to Us through Difficulties

"I used to wander off until you disciplined me;
but now I closely follow your word.
You are good and do only good; teach me your decrees."
—Psalm 119:67–68

*God whispers to us in our pleasures, speaks in our conscience, but shouts
in our pains: it is his megaphone to rouse a deaf world.*
—C. S. Lewis[1]

DOUG WAS A JOURNALER SCHEDULED FOR A PROSTATE BIOPSY AND was quite nervous about it. He didn't go through things like this very well. That morning he journaled his way through Luke 12:35–53. What struck him was that Jesus said that he didn't come just to bring peace but also tension. There would be curves in the road and he also knew that if we remain faithful and in touch with God, God would prove himself faithful in this trial. Journaling his way through this Scripture had encouraged him as he spent extra time with Jesus in prayer and meditation. He testified that he was able to go into the medical process with a more confident spirit, being assured that his heavenly Father was with him.

When I ask members of an audience to raise their hands if they've ever heard God speak to them when they were in difficulties, almost everyone raises their hands. All of us go through trials. Going through difficult times not only tests our values but also opens our ears to hear God's voice. Journaling can help you in this process. It's for real people who hurt and deal with difficulties.

PEARLS OF WISDOM

Rachel Naomi Remen is a medical specialist who serves individuals struggling with terminal cancer. She has an opportunity to listen to a lot of people. One of her favorite parables is "pearls of wisdom." She notes that an oyster is soft, tender, and vulnerable. Without the sanctuary of its shell, an oyster could not survive. But an oyster must also open its shell in order to "breathe" water. At times, when an oyster is breathing, a grain of sand will enter its shell and become part of its life from then on. It is not surprising that such grains of sand cause pain, but the oyster does not alter its soft nature because of this. It does not become hard and leathery in order not to feel pain. It continues to entrust itself to the ocean, to remain open and keep breathing. But it does respond. Slowly and patiently, the oyster wraps the grain of sand in thin translucent layers until, over time, it has created something of great value in the place where it was most vulnerable to pain. She notes that a pearl might be thought of as an oyster's response to its suffering. Not every oyster can do this. Oysters that do are far more valuable to people than oysters that don't.

It is obvious that sand is a way of life for an oyster. In the same way, difficulties are a way of life for us humans. These difficulties become opportunities for us to shape valuable pearls.[2]

THE STILL SMALL VOICE

Elijah, the prophet, also endured difficult times. There were euphoric experiences such as the one that he had on Mount Carmel when he saw God's fire come down from heaven and consume the sacrifice he had laid out before the Lord. On that great occasion, all the leaders of Israel shouted in response, "The LORD—he is God! Yes, the LORD is God!" (1 Kings 18:39). But this great victory soon turned into a time of deep depression for the prophet. Jezebel, the wicked queen, threatened to take his life by the next day. He felt lost and defeated.

In this troubled time, the Lord commanded Elijah to stand in his presence, for he himself would pass by. Elijah was to listen for God's voice. But what would it sound like?

"Then a great and powerful wind tore the mountains apart and shattered the rocks before the LORD, but the LORD was not in the wind. After the wind, there was an earthquake, but the LORD was not in the earthquake. After the earthquake came a fire, but the LORD was not in the fire. And after the fire came a gentle whisper" (1 Kings 19:11–12 NIV). It was through that gentle whisper (or "still small voice", as the phrase is translated in the King James Version) that God gave Elijah instructions for the next phase of his life.

We need to listen for God's gentle whisper when we encounter troubles and trials. The apostle James put it this way: "Dear brothers and sisters, whenever trouble comes your way, let it be an opportunity for joy. For when your faith is tested, your endurance has a chance to grow. So let it grow, for when your endurance is fully developed, you will be strong in character and ready for anything" (James 1:2–4). That is an amazing passage of Scripture!

An Invitation to Talk

David, the king, was often surrounded by difficulties. He learned how to hear God's voice during such times: "My heart has heard you say, 'Come and talk with me.' And my heart responds, 'LORD, I am coming'" (Ps. 27:8). Here was God's invitation to David in his tough times—to come and talk with him.

The Tough Thorn

Paul, the apostle, recalled a very painful problem, which he described as "a thorn in my flesh." Many have debated what the nature of that thorn was. Some argue that it may have been Paul's former wife. They base this on the theory that he had been a Pharisee and one from this religious order had to be married to hold that post. Others think that the thorn may have been dimness of vision, a physical malady such as malaria, or even a permanent disfigurement. Whatever it was, Paul was quite certain what the thorn represented: "a messenger from

Satan to torment me" (2 Cor. 12:7). The term "torment" literally means to "beat up." The picture is that of a boxer being pummeled senseless in a boxing ring. This gives us some idea of how Paul felt about this pain.

Sometimes we understand this and many times we don't. It gives us another reason to believe that God's desire for us is a relationship—to become real people of God. Why did such a terrible thing happen to such a faithful servant of God? As a matter of fact, it was difficult for Paul to understand it as well. There were times when this mighty man of prayer pleaded with the Lord to remove this thorn from his life. Each time, the Lord replied, "My grace is all you need. My power works best in weakness" (2 Cor. 12:9).

There it is—the whole reason God allowed the thorn in the first place! It was specifically designed to keep Paul humble and to bring him face to face with a new depth of weakness so that he might be thrust to a new height of grace. God spoke to Paul directly through his difficulties. Haven't you found it to be so in your life? God speaks to us most clearly in our pain. Journaling during such times of pain and uncertainty can be a conduit for our understanding and processing our experiences.

PREPARATION

The great preacher, Charles H. Spurgeon, understood this paradox. One of the weaknesses he struggled with his entire career was depression. There were occasions on which, after having preached on Sunday, he would go into his room and not come out until the middle of the week. He came to realize that depression came over him whenever the Lord was preparing him for a larger ministry with a greater degree of effectiveness.

CALL TO INTIMACY

Every difficulty that comes our way is "Father filtered." The Good Shepherd knows his sheep, and watches over them with tender care (John 10:1–15).

A lamb that is repeatedly lost, exposed to all sorts of dangers because of its waywardness, may find that the shepherd will purposefully break one of its legs. The shepherd then carries that lamb tenderly during the healing process. When that sheep is released from the arms of the shepherd to walk on its own again, it is not a surprise that that sheep will remain closer to the shepherd than any of the others in the flock. The pain and healing have bonded the sheep with the shepherd.

In the same way, difficulties are used to speak into our lives, to teach us lessons that can only be learned through times of trial and testing.

When was the last time you heard God speak to your life through difficulties? Don't waste the pain. Hear what God is saying to you and respond to him.

Record all of it in your journal. It will become your place of processing and clarifying what God is trying to communicate to you. Sometimes you have an insight that brings immediacy to your frustrations, other times it takes a longer period of time to begin to understand what God is saying to us personally. But in either case, it's worth being in God's presence journaling on such occasions.

REFLECTION QUESTIONS

1. Read Psalm 119:67–68: "I used to wander off until you disciplined me; but now I closely follow your word. You are good and do only good; teach me your decrees." What does this Scripture say? What do these verses mean for you?

2. Have you ever heard the Lord speak to you through difficulties? Why do we usually listen more intently to the Lord during tough times?

3. What does the parable of the oyster teach us? Have you experienced this process in your life?

4. Why did Paul have to live with a "thorn" in his flesh? What answer did Paul come to regarding God's purpose in this affliction?

5. Can you see how journaling will help you in processing life's difficulties?

6. Read James 1:2–4: "Dear brothers and sisters, whenever trouble comes your way, let it be an opportunity for joy. For when your faith is tested, your endurance has a chance to grow. So let it grow, for when your endurance is fully developed, you will be strong in character and ready for anything." Are difficulties just annoyances, or are they necessary in order for us to mature?

8

God Speaks to Us through His Creation

*The heavens proclaim the glory of God ... Day after day they continue to
speak; night after night they make him known.*
—Psalm 19:1–2

*Earth's crammed with heaven,
And every common bush afire with God;
But only he who sees takes off his shoes.*
—Elizabeth Barrett Browning[1]

CREATION REVEALS THE CREATOR

THE BIBLE MAKES THE POINT THAT GOD'S CREATION IS A MIRROR THAT reflects his invisible attributes. Paul writes that in creation all people "can clearly see his invisible qualities—his eternal power and divine nature. So they have no excuse whatsoever for not knowing God" (Rom. 1:20). In other words, the Creator has left clear markers in his handiwork that leave no doubt that he is the one who made it all. Think of it. God is continually reaching out and wanting a relationship with us! That makes us people who are real. We have a living God who speaks to us everyday.

Take a moment to reflect on the message God gives us through his design and care for the smallest bird in the world, the hummingbird. This bird weighs a mere one-tenth of an ounce and beats its wings up to eighty strokes per second. Aerodynamically, it has the ability to fly forward, backward, and sideways, and is also able to hover in one spot for minutes. Its heart beats up to 1,000 times per minute, and thus the hummingbird requires almost non-stop feeding. It is this need that makes its migration patterns astounding. This wonderfully engineered creature migrates up to 1,800 miles between Alaska and Hawaii. A hummingbird's tiny wings will beat more than two-and-one-half million times during this amazing journey. This small bird actually slows down its metabolism and hibernates every night in order to conserve energy. Just reflecting on the amazing energy God has put into this creature speaks volumes to us about the kind of God we have.[2]

NATURE IS GOD'S CLASSROOM

When Jesus taught his followers about the spiritual dimension of life, he repeatedly turned to his creation to make a point. This is scarcely surprising. After all, "Christ is the one through whom God created everything in heaven and earth" (Col. 1:16). Therefore, we can be certain that creation is full of embedded messages from Jesus.

On one occasion, when Jesus addressed the deep concern the people had for sufficient food, drink, and clothing, he encouraged his followers to look up and see what God was doing around them. He pointed to the birds of the air and said, "Look at the birds. They don't plant or harvest or store food in barns, for your heavenly Father feeds them" (Matt. 6:26). He was making a strong case that if God cares for the birds, how much more will he care for us, as we are more valuable than they.

LIFE PARABLES

Jesus routinely used parables from nature to clarify his teaching. I believe his Spirit also speaks to us in parable-like form today to give us instruction for our lives. Let me illustrate. While I was pastoring in Visalia, California, God gave me the following experience. It began when I found myself tired, discouraged, and in need of a word from the Lord. Yes, I had had my Bible reading time and I had done my journaling, but I sensed that the Spirit was drawing me to meet him in the outdoors. So I checked out of the office and found myself driving toward the small town of Three Rivers, which was nestled at the base of a mountain range. On an impulse, I turned onto a mountain road which paralleled a snow-fed stream. The road had a steep incline and many curves, but I was in no hurry; I was reflecting on meeting with the Lord.

Finally, I found an appropriate place to park and relax. I noticed that the stream I had been following was about thirty feet wide and didn't look too deep, so I took off my shoes and socks, rolled up my pant legs, and made my way to a boulder which looked like a suitable place to sit. Soon I was able to relax and drink in the beauty of the mountain setting.

It was then that I sensed the presence of the Lord ministering to me. This gave me the boldness to ask the Lord to speak to me. I wanted to have answers to certain questions I was dealing with, and wisdom to know how to lead the church to the next level. I really didn't know what to expect from the Lord by way of an answer. I had never quite asked for something this boldly and directly before.

Slowly I became aware of the melodic sound of the water striking the keys of thousands of river rocks as it flowed downstream. I sat there almost mesmerized by the music that rose from the river as the water crashed and bounced off the rocks.

Then, I heard God speak to my heart. I heard the Lord saying to me: "If there were no rocks in the river, there would be no music in the stream." So I listened again to the beautiful symphonic sounds coming out of the rock-filled stream. The application to me was that if there would be no difficulties in my life, there would be no music of God's grace resounding in my life either. I sat there in awe, reflecting on what the Spirit had just clarified in my heart. I then thanked God for the rocks that were strewn in my life and for how he would use them to bring music to the lives of the people around me. I will never forget that afternoon. We are changed when we hear God's voice.

Surely God's creation declares his glory and pours forth speech night after night, day after day. Surely God speaks to us through his creation. Therefore, I have found it to be a good thing to focus on some aspect of God's creation for at least thirty minutes each week. I urge you to do the same.

Reflect on the song penned by C. Austin Miles in 1912:

I come to the garden alone,
While the dew is still on the roses,
And the voice I hear, falling on my ear,
The Son of God discloses.

And he walks with me and he talks with me,
And he tells me I am his own,
And the joy we share, as we tarry there,
None other has ever known.

He speaks, and the sound of his voice
Is so sweet the birds hush their singing
And the melody that he gave to me
Within my heart is ringing.

And he walks with me and he talks with me,
And he tells me I am his own,
And the joy we share, as we tarry there,
None other has ever known.[3]

REFLECTION QUESTIONS

1. Read Psalm 19:1–2: "The heavens proclaim the glory of God. The skies display his craftsmanship. Day after day they continue to speak; night after night they make him known." How does nature declare the glory of God, speak, and make God known? Give some examples.

2. Why do people "have no excuse" regarding knowing the truth of God (Rom. 1:20)? What is the underlying principle of God's relationship with people?

3. What is a parable? Why did Jesus use so many parables in his teaching?

4. When have you heard God speak to you through his creation? Why could it prove helpful to intentionally focus on creation on a regular basis?

5. Elizabeth Barrett Browning wrote: "Earth's crammed with heaven and every common bush afire with God; but only he who sees takes off his shoes." What is Browning saying?

9

God Speaks to Us through Circumstances

And we know that God causes everything to work together for the good of those who love God and are called according to his purpose for them.
—Romans 8:28

The key to understanding our circumstances is to focus on Christ rather than our circumstances.
—Henry and Richard Blackaby[1]

THE SCRIPTURES ASSURE US THAT GOD IS THE LORD OF PURPOSE AND design. He causes all things to work together for good. But our circumstances can be confusing and not always readily understood. As a matter of fact, it may take years until we catch on to what God was doing in a particular situation; yet, in retrospect, we see how it all turned out for good.

Life is really one big set of circumstances. Circumstances can take many shapes. They include our health and our work. They include simple things such as a phone call or an e-mail message that surprises us. They include important issues such as marriage, family, and friends, which engage us in different ways during different seasons of our life. And, of course, there are things that hit us quite suddenly, such as a death, a car accident, an unexpected gift, a surprise visit, a miraculous recovery, or an unusual conversation. Daily we are inundated by various circumstances that we have to think through. It is so beneficial to have a vehicle like journaling to process the myriad things we face on a daily basis.

God does speak to us through these happenings. Yet, many of these situations we don't think through carefully because there are too many of them or they are too confusing. In this section, we will focus on circumstances as being happenings that are orchestrated by God to speak to us about himself and his will. Certainly there are times when I have grappled with what God's orchestrating in my life. I have recorded some of my frustrations. It helps me to identify what part of my faith I'm struggling with. People around me can tell that I am a real person. I also have my ups and downs! Strange as it may seem, this can be a comfort to many.

FOCUSING ON GOD

When God led his people Israel out of Egypt, it was with great power and miracles. This should have left little doubt in this nation of newly released slaves that it was the God of their forefathers who had done the miracles. They were, however, still shallow in their understanding and obedience toward God. For this reason, God put them through further trying circumstances in order that they would be able to witness both his power and wisdom. The entire set of circumstances was designed to teach them to put their full trust in him.

In their flight from Egypt, the Israelites were caught in a humanly impossible situation. Before them was the Red Sea; to the right was a flaming desert; to the left was a range of mountains; and biting at their heels was Pharaoh's crack military machine. Humanly speaking, the position was untenable; the Israelites could neither defend themselves nor escape.

In these circumstances, Moses called the people to not be afraid, but rather to wait and see what the Lord their God would do. The message was simple, but clear: "The LORD himself will fight for you. You won't have to lift a finger in your defense" (Ex. 14:14). Then, God, before their very eyes, separated the sea so they could cross over to the other side. Not only was Israel saved from the spears of the Egyptians, but also the mighty army of Pharaoh was routed by God as the sea collapsed upon his soldiers. The result was that the people "feared the LORD and put their faith in him and his servant Moses" (Ex. 14:31). A significant principle surfaces in this story—that our focus should remain on God during difficult circumstances since he alone can save us!

A PERSONAL STORY

The first pastoral experience for Carol and me was in Sawyer, North Dakota. We came out of Bible college and were prepared to test our ministry wings in this wonderful, caring congregation. After five years of ministry in this country church, God increasingly gave me the desire to go on to further studies in seminary to strengthen my pastoral and ministry skills. By this time, we had two children, and the third was on his way. It was in this context that we began serious talk of attending seminary. We felt confident that God was calling us in this direction. Our problem, however, was that we were short of funds. Basically, we were living "hand to mouth." How then could I afford to give up my job and go back to school?

About four months prior to our planned move to Fresno, California, God gave us a unique experience. A Mr. Newman, who was a member of the local Pentecostal church, had the ill fortune of having his house burn down. Several weeks after this catastrophe, he came to visit us at our parsonage and shared with us a dream that he had received from the Lord—that I would build him a new house. I hesitated, knowing that it had been a number of years since I had worked in construction with my father, who had been a contractor. Mr. Newman informed me that he had already spoken with our church moderator and had the assurance that I would be released for this project as long as I continued to take care of the preaching ministry on the weekend. So I hired a crew, lined up the sub-trades, and began building the house. It was amazing; in two-and-a-half months the house was totally constructed and ready for occupancy.

I'll always remember Mr. Newman's writing out a check that turned out to be sufficient for our move to California and for the first semester of seminary. God had used some interesting circumstances to confirm our call to graduate school and continued ministry. This made an impression on me that will last my whole life. Here were circumstances that in and of themselves may not have seemed good, but God was at work making the outcome good. This assurance is what holds me.

THROWING OUT A FLEECE

Gideon was called by God to deliver Israel from their arch-enemy, the Midianites (Judg. 6). Gideon, however, was uncertain that he was hearing from the Lord and was more than a little fearful of the whole enterprise. So he asked God to confirm his call to lead Israel into battle. How did he do it? He laid a fleece, a piece of sheepskin, out on the ground one evening and asked that God would make it totally wet with dew and keep the ground around it dry. The next morning, to his surprise, the fleece was wet and the ground remained dry. But he still had his doubts, so he asked God that the next night the fleece would remain dry and the grass around it would be wet. Again, God graciously did as Gideon requested. In this way, he received the necessary assurance to lead God's people into battle. Gideon won great battles by heeding God's voice in his planning.

It is important to remember that God is not compelled to repeat the fleece miracle in our own experience. God can communicate his will through various circumstances. However, I do believe we can ask God to confirm his word in our lives so that we can be assured that we are doing his will. But we must leave the methodology up to him. He will often surprise us with the way he answers. He is a God who communicates in such a way as to display his character. Journaling may help in bringing pieces together to see if God is truly responding to our fleece.

INTRODUCING JESUS

The Gospel of John identifies the miracles of Jesus as "signs." The first of these signs was at Cana in Galilee, where Jesus attended a wedding and turned water into wine. Why did Jesus do this miracle? The Gospel says, "This miraculous sign at Cana in Galilee was Jesus' first display of his glory. And his disciples believed in him" (John 2:11). The sign communicated a powerful message of who Jesus is.

Often, after sharing the Gospel with someone, I ask a question something like this: "Could you believe that God may have arranged our meeting today for the specific reason of informing you about how you could get to know him personally?" More often than not, there is a positive response. God can use the circumstances of a meeting we hadn't planned on as a divine appointment.

PRINCIPLES THAT HELP US EMBRACE OUR CIRCUMSTANCES

1. God loves you. "Overwhelming victory is ours through Christ, who loved us. And I am convinced that nothing can ever separate us from God's love" (Rom. 8:37–38). When we begin with the fact that God loves us unconditionally, we have a solid understanding from which to begin working our way through the circumstances that we encounter from day to day.

2. The Holy Spirit teaches us. In the midst of your specific circumstances, be confident of Jesus' promise that the Holy Spirit "will teach you everything and will remind you of everything I myself have told you" (John 14:26). The ministry of the Holy Spirit is significant as we work our way through understanding our circumstances.

3. The church community is filled with godly wisdom. The various gifts that are expressed in the church can speak insight into our lives. We are admonished to seek godly wisdom because "There is safety in having many advisers" (Prov. 11:14).

4. Those who are patient will experience God's promise of peace. The Lord assures us with these words: "Be still in the presence of the LORD, and wait patiently for him to act" (Ps. 37:7). Remember that even though not everything is or seems good, our Father is the one who promises to work all things out for good as we follow his voice.

Listen to the story that was communicated to me. "When I learned about journaling, my heart jumped because as a new Christian in the '70s I had learned to journal and had gotten away from it. This brought back memories of how real the Lord was in me then and how I had grown in that period of time, so I began to journal for myself. It came at a time when I really needed strength and courage. I can't even explain how many times, as I spent time with him, how he helped me through a difficult period. My dad passed away on June 12. The night before my husband was able to lead him to the Lord, and this was what I was so praying for. I had been so afraid that my dad would not respond and he was running out of time. But my journaling helped me focus on God." This testimony gives evidence of what can happen to you as a real person, as you face real problems.

REFLECTION QUESTIONS

1. Romans 8:28: "And we know that God causes everything to work together for the good of those who love God and are called according to his purpose for them." Is everything "good" that comes into your life? What is our part in recognizing that all things work together for good? What is God's part?

2. What circumstances are you facing today that are difficult? What can help you see God's incredible love in this situation?

3. Why were Moses and the Israelites placed in an impossible circumstance by the Lord? What does this say to us today?

4. Does God use the same methodology in each situation today to build up our faith in him? Why or why not?

5. What principles can help us embrace our unique set of circumstances?

6. Do you agree with Blackaby that "The key to understanding our circumstances is to focus on Christ rather than our circumstances"?

10

God Speaks to Us through Angels

Angels are only servants, spirits sent to care for people who will inherit salvation.
—Hebrews 1:14

Angels minister to us personally.
—Billy Graham[1]

THE TERM "ANGEL" LITERALLY MEANS "MESSENGER." ANGELS ARE A special order of God's creation to serve those who will receive salvation. Whether we are aware of it or not, God communicates to us through angels.

Currently people are fascinated with angels. They have become objects of much attention on calendars, jewelry, statuettes, and stationery. Charles Stanley warns: "Many people today have been duped into thinking that they can call on angels or conjure them up. They may be conjuring spirits all right, but let me assure you, the visages of them are not God's angels. God's angels come to people uninvited, unannounced, and unexpected."[2]

Angels appeared to men and women throughout Old and New Testament times. This whole book could be devoted to just the study of angels. However, we will look at only a few of the remarkable cases of angels appearing in the Bible.

THE EXPERIENCE OF ISRAEL

Jacob's experience with angels is a splendid example of angels ministering to God's people. Jacob did not deserve nor expect the ministry of angels. He had schemed to steal the birthright from his brother Esau, had lied to his father Isaac, and was now on the run from his older brother, fleeing to save his life. Suddenly he found himself alone and no doubt totally confused. In this state of desolation, he lay down with a stone as his pillow. It was then that God gave him a marvelous dream of "a stairway that reached from the earth up to heaven. And he saw the angels of God going up and down on the stairway" (Gen. 28:12).

The Lord declared to him, "I am the LORD, the God of your grandfather Abraham and the God of your father, Isaac" (Gen. 28:13). Then God renewed his covenant with an undeserving recipient with the words: "Your descendents will be as numerous as the dust of the earth! They will cover the land from east to west and from north to south. All the families of the earth will be blessed through you and your descendants" (Gen. 28:14). Is this not a wonderful picture of God's ministry to Jacob through his holy angels? They would be ascending and descending from heaven all the days of his life, blessing, encouraging, and helping him to make all this a reality.

Over four hundred years later, Jacob's descendants were caught in the pain and drudgery of enslavement in Egypt. They cried out to God for help. In response, God raised up Moses for the awesome task of releasing the slaves from Pharaoh's crushing grip. The process was long and trying, but finally, in God's timing, Israel was released, and the Israelites began their long march into freedom. A short commentary on this huge event is recorded in the book of Numbers: "But when we cried out to the LORD, he heard us and sent an angel who brought us out of Egypt" (Num. 20:16). Now, isn't that remarkable? There was an invisible dimension of warfare going on, and God sent an angel to make sure that the warfare was accomplished successfully.

ANGELS PROCLAIMED JESUS

In the New Testament, we are again introduced to the angel Gabriel. He was sent to bring a significant message to Zechariah—that his wife Elizabeth would bear a son, his name would be John, and he would prepare the way for the Messiah (Luke 1:11–17). Only a few months later, Gabriel was given an assignment which must have been awesome for him to speak. He brought a message to Mary that she would bear a son whose name would be Jesus, for he would be the Savior of the world (Luke 1:26–33). Nine months later, at the birth of Jesus, the angel of the Lord and myriads of other angels joined in praise to God, who had sent the Savior (Luke 2:8–14).

Later, when Jesus was in the wilderness being tempted by the evil one, angels came to minister to him (Matt. 4:11). And, on that great resurrection morning, the angel of the Lord rolled the stone away from the grave, sat upon it, and said to the disciples, "Why are you looking among the dead for someone who is alive?" (Luke 24:5). Again, the angels were messengers of God.

In the growth of the early church, angels were God's servants in answering prayer, launching evangelistic initiatives, and opening doors for ministry. Once, when Paul was lost at sea, God sent an angel to comfort him and tell him, "Don't be afraid, Paul, for you will surely stand trial before Caesar! What's more, God in his goodness has granted safety to everyone sailing with you" (Acts 27:24). Everything God promised through his angel occurred as the angel had said.

ANGELS TODAY

Does God still speak through angels? It is encouraging to realize that, "Jesus Christ is the same yesterday, today, and forever" (Heb. 13:8).

Billy Graham's wife, Ruth, born and raised in China, recalled that in her childhood, tigers lived in the mountains. One day, a poor woman went up to the foothills to cut grass. To her back was tied a baby, and a little child walked beside her. In her hand she carried a sharp sickle to cut the grass. Just as she reached the top of the hill, she heard a roar. Frightened and almost speechless, she looked around to see a mother tigress springing at her. This illiterate Chinese mother had never attended school or entered a church. She had never seen a Bible. But a year or two earlier a missionary had told her about Jesus. She remembered him saying that Jesus is "able to help when you are in trouble." As the claws of the tiger tore her arm and shoulder, the woman cried out in a frenzy, "Oh, Jesus, help me!" The ferocious beast, instead of attacking again to get an easy meal, suddenly turned and ran away. This incident reminded

Graham of Psalm 91:11, "He will order his angels to protect you wherever you go." Had God sent an angel to help this poor Chinese peasant woman? Are there supernatural beings who still influence the affairs of men and nations?[3]

Peter Marshall, the Scotsman who in the middle of the twentieth century became one of America's most widely acclaimed ministers, was known for a number of qualities. He was a great orator, and this brought him to the office of chaplain of the United States Senate. Back in Scotland one foggy, pitch-black Northumberland night he was taking a shortcut across the moors, in an area where there were deep, deserted limestone quarries.

As he plodded blindly forward, an urgent voice called out, "Peter."

He stopped and answered, "Yes, who is it? What do you want?" But there was no response.

Thinking he was mistaken, he took a few more steps. The voice came again, even more urgently: "Peter!" At this, he stopped again, and, trying to peer ahead in the darkness, stumbled and fell on his knees. Putting down his hand to brace himself, he found nothing there. As he felt around in a semicircle, he discovered that he was right on the brink of an abandoned quarry; one step more would certainly have killed him. Had God sent one of his holy angels to shout his name?[4]

In every church I have served as pastor, individuals have come to me at various times and shared that they have seen angels in the service during the time of ministry. In questioning these individuals more closely, I came to the realization that these visions were usually during times of spiritual warfare. It appeared that the Lord opened the eyes of certain people to see that there was a powerful spiritual battle taking place as the worship service was going on. Those who informed me of these visions were believable, wise, and solid Christians.

We are being ministered to moment by moment by God's holy angels. At times, God uses angels to bring us a message. After all, angel means "messenger". As you keep your spiritual eyes and ears open, there are times you will receive messages from people or protection in critical situations that will be done by God's messengers, his holy angels.

REFLECTION QUESTIONS

1. Read Hebrews 1:14: "Angels are only servants, spirits sent from God to care for people who will inherit salvation." What do these Scriptures teach us about the ministry of angels? (Also see Heb. 13:1–2: "Continue to love each other with true Christian love. Don't forget to show hospitality to strangers, for some who have done this have entertained angels without realizing it!")

2. How were angels involved in Jacob's life? In the great Exodus story?

3. How were angels involved in Jesus' life? What does this teach us?

4. Does God still speak through angels? Are we always aware of angels working in our life? (Heb. 13:1–2).

5. Do you believe that God sends angels to minister to you daily? Can you recount a time where you have been aware that angels were serving you or others around you?

11

God Speaks to Us By Giving Us Blessings

Every good and perfect gift is from above, coming down from the Father.
—James 1:17 NIV

God gives where he finds empty hands.
—St. Augustine[1]

GOD HAS GIVEN US SEVEN THOUSAND PROMISES IN THE SCRIPTURES. The writer John in his gospel exclaims, "We have all benefited from the rich blessings he brought to us—one gracious blessing after another" (John 1:16). A wonderful method God uses to get our attention and speak to us is by giving us gifts or blessings. At times these may be unexpected, and on other occasions they may come as a response to a specific prayer. In either case, it encourages our hearts to experience the special love God has for us.

The Scriptures remind us that "God is love" (1 John 4:16). Our heavenly Father is not just loving, but love. Love is not first of all a description of God, but it is the essence of who he is. And giving is a genuine demonstration of love. Therefore, to say that God loves is to say that he gives! The blessings he gives may be spiritual or material, financial or physical. Whatever they are, they are intended to help us hear the gracious voice of our heavenly Father saying, "I love you. I enjoy giving you blessings." Paul, filled with the Spirit, declared, "All praise to God, the Father of our Lord Jesus Christ, who has blessed us with every spiritual blessing in the heavenly realms because we are united with Christ" (Eph. 1:3).

Do we recognize God's voice when we receive the gifts of encouragement or affirmation? Do we sense the Father's joy when we receive an unexpected financial gift or a set of tickets to see a hockey game? Do we hear God celebrating with us when we move into a new house or drive in a shiny new or pre-owned car? It is a wonderful thing to keep a record of the special gifts God gives because, through them, he speaks.

I'm sure each of us has memories of special gifts God has presented to us as reminders of his delight in us. I can recall a building contractor inviting me to his job site and showing me a new apartment complex he had just completed. I was interested, listened carefully, and asked questions. I was impressed with his building skills. After the tour of the site was complete, he pulled an envelope out of his jacket pocket and said, "This is for you."

To my complete surprise, it was an invitation for Carol and me to join him and his wife on an all-expenses-paid trip to Hawaii. After I got over some of my shock, he told me a story. During the construction of this complex he received the idea from the Lord that he should do something special for his pastor. He made an agreement with God that if there was a certain amount of profit in the job, he would carry through on this resolve. "Well," he said, "to my surprise, when the project was finished and my accountant did the books, there was twice as much profit in the job as I had anticipated! So, I had no choice but to follow through on my agreement with the Lord." In the following weeks, Carol and I had lots of fun preparing for and anticipating this wonderful vacation. It was a gift from God.

It is important for us to remember that we cannot exhaust God's capacity to give. At times we may impede it, but we can never exhaust it.

We do well also to recognize a basic principle God has put in place for us to follow: "Give and you will receive. Your gift will return to you in full measure, pressed down, shaken together to make room for more, running over. Whatever measure you use in giving—large or small—it will be used to measure what is to be given back to you"

(Luke 6:38). What Jesus was teaching us is that for the harvest of blessings to continue, we must become like God in giving generously.

God's blessings speak to us. They are also meant to draw us into an intimate relationship with our heavenly Father: "Or do you show contempt for the riches of his kindness, tolerance and patience, not realizing that God's kindness leads you toward repentance?" (Rom. 2:4 NIV). Ask yourself, "What blessings is God sending my way?" and "What is he saying to me?"

REFLECTION QUESTIONS

1. Read James 1:17: "Whatever is good and perfect comes to us from God above, who created all heaven's lights. Unlike them, he never changes or casts shifting shadows." How do we know that God loves to give blessings to us?

2. When you receive a gift from a friend, what message can that gift carry with it? Give an example.

3. Does God love to give? How do you know that?

4. What basic principle of "giving and receiving" has God put in place in his kingdom?

5. Romans 2:4 asks, "Do you show contempt for the riches of his kindness, tolerance and patience, not realizing that God's kindness leads you toward repentance?" (NIV). What is the kindness of God leading us to in our spiritual lives?

12

Journaling: My Life Travelogue

Jesus often withdrew to the wilderness for prayer.
—Luke 5:16

*Learn to listen to God. If you do you are in for an incredible journey,
and you will soon have your own stories of divine appointments to tell.
Because, you see, listening is for life—both here on earth and in eternity.*
—Marilyn Hontz[1]

JOURNALING IS A PRACTICE THAT WILL DEMAND DISCIPLINE, BUT IT will reward you with blessings beyond your expectations. I have discovered in my twenty-five years of journaling that our Creator God reveals his message to us like a diamond, always refracting himself to us with fresh insights and experiences. Some days are more engaging than others, but if we seek him every day, we will always have an intimate time with God which will prepare us for the day ahead. This nurturing connection with God will usher us into a life of godly confidence and expectation. Solitude with God gives us the quiet strength to live joyfully and serve humbly in our public worlds.

It is always a delight to see a man and woman who are truly in love. They are attentive to one another, laugh a lot, and dream together. So it is also with us and our loving Savior. The Scriptures remind us that God loves us with an everlasting love, and he calls us to love him with all of our heart, mind, soul, and strength. The joy of such love is infectious and engaging. I believe that journaling can move us out of the spectator role into the participant role. God calls us to participate with him in the great work of his kingdom.

We know the Bible exhorts us to always be in an attitude of prayer (1 Thess. 5:17), but too often we miss out on intimate times with our heavenly Father. The Scriptures provide a wonderful commentary about King David's experience: "Then King David went in and sat before the LORD and prayed" (2 Sam. 7:18). How often have you just simply sat before God and waited on him? David did! And Jesus did! Jesus had the Spirit of God without measure and yet found himself again and again waiting before his heavenly Father for instructions. We also read that "Jesus often withdrew to the wilderness for prayer" (Luke 5:16). For our Savior, this time with his Father was not an option; rather, it was critical in order for him to stay on track with his calling and mission. How much more is it necessary for us to grow in our connection with God?

In the initial part of this book, I related some of my own experiences as I began the practice of journaling. Next, I identified eight primary ways in which God speaks to us. At the heart of all these various ways that God communicates is the Bible, the living Word of God. For this reason, reading and meditating on the Word is key to journaling and hearing God's voice. Next, I identified six ways to test an impression, prompting or vision, as to whether it is from God or not.

By now, you may be convinced that journaling is something you want to do, something you need to do. But how do you begin? In the following pages, I will walk with you as you start out along a journaling path. More precisely, I will give you six practical steps intended to answer the question: "How do I journal?"

1. WITHDRAW: FIND A PLACE OF SOLITUDE

In the busy, noisy traffic of life, we seldom find solitude, and often we are afraid of it. Jesus models for us ways to build our public ministry (the areas where we work and serve God) around regular times of solitude. At the outset of his ministry, he spent forty days by himself in the desert (Matt. 4:1–11). When the time came for him to choose his disciples, he spent a whole night alone on a mountaintop praying (Luke 6:12). Again, when Jesus received the news of John the

Baptist's death, "he went off by himself in a boat to a remote area to be alone" (Matt. 14:13). In another location, he invited three disciples to the silence of a lonely mountain as the platform for a memorable transfiguration (Matt. 17:1–9). Again, he prepared himself for his passion in the stillness of Gethsemane (Matt. 26:36–46). These are but a sample of the many times Jesus withdrew to pray. The point is clear. If we want to follow Jesus, we will have to take regular times to be with our heavenly Father in prayer.

a. What can this time alone look like?

Find a place where you can withdraw to pray and journal. It is always a challenge to find such a place, whether you are married or single. Such a place in your home should have a comfortable chair, plenty of light, and enough seclusion that you won't be interrupted. It will take discipline on your part and understanding on the part of your family.

At least once a month, I suggest you get out of your house or apartment and journal away from home. I often journal by parking my car near a lake or a place where there is a vision of a valley or a mountain. There may also be the possibility that you could spend this time in a church prayer room or at a retreat center. During this special time of journaling, you may want to review what God is doing in your life, your family, and your job—and/or explore different ways that God has been speaking to you. This usually proves to be a very refreshing time.

b. What should I bring?

Very simply, bring your Bible, your journal, a pen, and a highlighter. I usually bring a glass of water as well—it is a reminder to me of the refreshing that Christ gives me through his living water. Most important, bring an open heart and mind. Ask the Spirit to give you his sense of anticipation. The Psalmist expresses it well:

> "As a deer longs for streams of water,
> so I long for you, O God.
> I thirst for God, the living God.
> When can I go and stand before him?"
> (Psalm 42:1–2)

2. WAIT: RELAX YOUR THOUGHTS AND EMOTIONS

"Be still in the presence of the LORD,
and wait patiently for him to act."
(Psalm 37:7)

Most often, it takes me a few minutes to relax. If I don't con-
sciously relax, I find that journaling is a task rather than a delight.
Here are a few suggestions that you may want to use from time to
time.

Breathe deeply, and enjoy a glass of water. Allow the breathing in
and breathing out to remind you of prayer, and the water to remind
you of the refreshing that you are anticipating in God's presence.

You may wish to stretch out your arms, turn your hands down-
ward and close them. Remain in that position for a few moments and
think of the anxieties, pressures and weights that you are carrying
right now. Cast these cares on Jesus, for he will care for you (1 Peter
5:7). He has been waiting for this special time with you. Now you
may wish to raise your hands and symbolically reach out to God as he
is reaching into your life.

Most often, I use these two verses as an introduction for my journaling time:

"Open my eyes to see
The wonderful truths in your instructions."
(Psalm 119:18)

"My sheep listen to my voice;
I know them, and they follow me.
I give them eternal life, and they will never perish.
No one can snatch them away from me."
(John 10: 27–28)

3. WATCH: INVITE GOD TO SPEAK TO YOU

Now that you are more relaxed and have prepared yourself to
hear from the Lord, you can open your Bible and read from the

Scriptures. Something quite remarkable happens when we open the Bible and begin reading it. Paul says it well in this prayer of his: "I pray that your hearts will be flooded with light so that you can understand the wonderful future he has promised to those he called" (Eph. 1:18).

a. What should I read?

If you are just beginning to journal through the Scriptures, a good starting place is the Gospel of Mark. Following that, I suggest you read one of the letters of Paul and then move to an Old Testament book such as Psalms. Remember, this is not first of all a heavy-duty Bible study time or a read-through-the-Bible-in-a-year program. These are excellent disciplines of a different sort. In journaling, we are looking for a time of meditation and spiritual formation.

b. How much should I read?

Most of the Bibles we use today have the text divided according to theme or story line. These dividers are good indicators of the amount you will want to read at a given time. Rather than going for an amount, go for depth. This may be contrary to what you've been taught. You can relax, enjoy, and go deep with the Lord. This is for real people.

Read your Scripture several times and ask the Spirit to highlight the verses that are for you today. As a rule of thumb, read until the Lord speaks to you through his Word. I have found it remarkable how the Spirit connects with my spirit as I follow this discipline.

4. Weed: Keep the Garden of Your Heart Clean

After reading the Scriptures is a timely occasion to examine the garden of your heart. I simply ask myself: "Is there a sin to confess or a hardness of my heart that needs softening?"

In the parable of the soil and the seed, which is recorded in all three synoptic Gospels, Jesus looked into the eyes of his listeners and declared, "Anyone with ears to hear should listen and understand" (Mark 4:9). Jesus compared the condition of a garden to the condition of people's hearts and their readiness to listen to God. One person had a hard heart, the next a shallow heart, and another a weed-infested heart. Because of these conditions, none of them was ready to receive God's message.

Tending the soil of the heart includes keeping the heart pure so the listener can see God (Matt. 5:8). It is sobering to read: "If I had not confessed the sin in my heart, the Lord would not have listened. But God did listen!" (Ps. 66:18–19).

If you find you have a sin that occurs in your life regularly, it is helpful to write it down on paper. Ask yourself: Does Christ have the power for me to overcome this sin? What promise in the Bible can I claim for this victory? How will I celebrate as God gives me the victory? These are very helpful questions to answer as you work through areas of personal weakness and sin.

When the soil of the heart is good, then the good seed, the Word of God, will reproduce and multiply thirty times, sixty times, even a hundred times. Here lies the secret of growing and celebrating the Christian life.

5. WRITE: RECORD YOUR CONVERSATION WITH THE LORD.

a. Begin by writing out the key Scripture verse(s) which you underlined in your Bible reading today.
It may be one verse or two verses or parts of several verses. You will find that writing out the Scriptures helps impress them on your mind and makes it easier for you to recall them during the rest of the day. God commanded the prophet Jeremiah to do this: "Write down for the record everything I have said to you" (Jer. 30:2).

b. Write down the insights you have received from reading your key Scriptures.
Ask yourself:
- What did I learn about God, Jesus, or the Holy Spirit?
- Is there a warning or a sin that I need to be aware of?
- Is there an invitation to receive?
- Is there an encouragement for me?
- Is there a command to follow?

These insights will help you to shape your prayer and your listening to God. I don't write paragraphs, but one-line insights. Doing this can help you to focus your attention on what God is saying.

c. Write down a conversational prayer.

Begin experimenting with recording a dialogical prayer with God. For example, write out in a sentence or two a prayer to God. Then become quiet and listen for the Spirit's promptings or impressions in your heart. Write them down. It may very well be God speaking to you.

I recall the first time I went through this exercise. I was tentative, but soon I had a heart filled with joy as I recognized God's speaking to me. He had done it before, but I simply had not fully recognized what he was doing.

By writing and listening, listening and writing, you can begin a chat with God. Mind you, all of this must be based on the Scriptures and the principles that were explained earlier in this book. If you are using our journaling book, never feel constrained by the amount of room on a certain page. You will soon discover that "Writing is thinking. Writing is clarifying. Writing is sifting out the most important issues. Writing is a boost to meditation and prayer" (Gordon MacDonald).

6. WORSHIP: LET GOD KNOW YOU LOVE HIM

The Westminster Catechism sums up God's invitation to us in a simple yet profound way: "The chief end and duty of man is to love God and to enjoy him forever." This includes worship. If you have connected with God, you will have a heart that is ready to worship. I suggest that you try the following exercise with your journal in hand:

- Read to the Lord the Scripture you have written in your journal.
- Thank God for the insights he gave you as you reflected on the Scriptures.
- Pray the dialogical prayer that you have inscribed in your journal. No doubt you will want to go beyond that prayer as the Holy Spirit inspires you in your prayer time.
- Pray for those who are on your prayer list and the special needs that you have noted in that section of your journal.

The invitation is clear and inviting:

"Come, let us worship and bow down.
Let us kneel before the LORD our maker,
for he is our God.
We are the people he watches over,
The flock under his care."
(Psalm 95:6–7)

Previously I have given you ideas of how God speaks. Now I hope that journaling will become a tool in helping you process what God is saying.

Join me in this journey!

(In the appendix is a journaling plan.)

REFLECTION QUESTIONS

1. What are some of the "unexpected" blessings God has given you when you set time aside to communicate with him?

2. How is the love of a man and woman a good picture of our relationship with our heavenly Father?

3. Where is the best place for you to withdraw to and be with the Lord? Do you believe the Lord will be there waiting for you?

4. How do you see yourself becoming still before the Lord and leaving behind the pressures of the day? How much time are you setting aside for your devotions? Are you going to change that?

5. Where do you plan to begin your Bible reading? Why?

6. How important is it to weed the garden of your heart daily? Why?

7. Why is it helpful to write out the Scripture which you have identified is God's Word for you today?

8. What is an insight? How can this help you in writing out your prayer?

9. Why is worship important in your inner life with God?

10. What is the next step you plan to take to begin or renew your journaling time with the Lord? To whom will you be accountable?

Appendix A

Prayer Journal

"Open my eyes that I may see wonderful things in your law."
Psalm 119:18*

"My sheep listen to my voice ... and they follow me."
John 10:27 (NLT)

Name:

Starting Date:

Completion Date:

* Unless otherwise noted, all scriptural references are quoted from the New International Version of the Bible.

Mapping your Prayer Journal

Introduction

WELCOME TO THE JOY OF JOURNALING. IT WAS OVER TWENTY-FIVE years ago that I made the discovery of keeping a record of my Scripture reading and prayers before the Lord. The Lord used the passionate testimony of Bill Hybels to invite me on this spiritual adventure. Listen to these words from one of his books:

> "Authentic Christians are persons who stand apart from others, even other Christians, as though listening to a different drummer. Their character seems deeper, their ideas fresher, their spirits softer, their courage greater, their convictions wider, their compassions more genuine, their conviction more concrete. They are joyful in spite of difficulties and show wisdom beyond their years."[1]

Some significant surprises came my way as I became involved in journaling. For one, I realized that what I was writing might actually be what God desired to communicate to me. I not only heard His words of discipline but even more significantly, His voice of love and hope. I experienced a new dimension of joy and intimacy with my heavenly Father.

Journaling, however, is both a discipline and a delight. Most people who begin journaling give up too soon. It takes about a year to develop this habit and make it a part of your faith and prayer lifestyle. The delight enters when we hear the voice of God in our hearts and are able to develop a consistent and growing prayer life. I am grateful to authors/teachers such as Roger Barrier, Wayne Cordeiro, Bill Hybels, Gordon MacDonald, John Piper and Rick Warren who have helped shape my journaling development. Their writing, teaching and passion has done much to impact my thinking and practice.

Does my wife read my journal? I doubt it! My handwriting is so poor she would have difficulty deciphering everything I record. You may discover that as you begin journaling you feel somewhat self-conscious and vulnerable as you write your thoughts. You need to realize that you are not surprising your heavenly Father. As a matter of fact, you will find occasions when you will address fears and hopes in your life that have been a part of your hidden self for a long time. Your Abba Father will speak peace into your heart.

The words of Jesus are powerful, "My sheep recognize my voice. I know them, and they follow me. I give them real and eternal life." John 10:27 (MSG)

I invite you onto this journey of discovery and growth.

Sincerely,
Vern Heidebrecht

1. Bill Hybels, *Too Busy Not to Pray* (Ill.: Intervarsity Press, 1988), 99

Seven Keys to Recognizing God's Voice

KEY 1: IS IT CONSISTENT WITH THE BIBLE?

"Heaven and earth will disappear, but my words will remain forever." Luke 21:33 (NLT)

KEY 2: DOES IT MAKE ME MORE LIKE JESUS?

"For God knew his people in advance, and he chose them to become like his son." Romans 8:29 (NLT)

KEY 3: DOES IT CHALLENGE ME TO BECOME STRONGER IN FAITH?

"We live by believing and not by seeing." 2 Corinthians 5:7 (NLT) "Faith comes from hearing the Good News about Christ." Romans 10:17 (NLT) "It is impossible to please God without faith." Hebrews 11:6 (NLT)

KEY 4: DOES MY CHURCH FAMILY CONFIRM IT?

"If two of you agree here on earth concerning anything you ask, my Father in heaven will do it for you. For where two or three gather together as my followers, I am there among them." Matthew 18:19–20

KEY 5: DOES IT CALL FOR COURAGE?

"This is my command—be strong and courageous! Do not be afraid or discouraged. For the LORD your God is with you wherever you go." Joshua 1:9 (NLT)

KEY 6: DO I SENSE GOD'S PEACE?

"You will experience God's peace, which exceeds anything we can understand. His peace will guard your hearts and minds as you live in Christ Jesus." Philippians 4:7 (NLT)

KEY 7: DOES IT CALL FOR HUMILITY?

"He leads the humble in doing right, teaching them his way." Psalm 25:9

LEARNING TO RECOGNIZE FALSE VOICES

- The Voice of Self
- The Voice of Satan

Journaling: Keeping a Record

PRIMARY WAYS GOD SPEAKS TO US

1. God Speaks Through the Bible

"Every part of Scripture is God-breathed and useful in one way or another—showing us truth, exposing our rebellion, correcting our mistakes, training us to live God's way."

2 Timothy 3:16 (MSG)

2. God Speaks Through Impressions of the Holy Spirit

"The Holy Spirit ... will teach you all things and will remind you of everything I have said to you."

John 14:26 (NIV)

3. God Speaks Through People

"So faith comes from hearing, that is, hearing the Good News about Christ."

Romans 10:17

4. God Speaks To Us Through Difficulties

"Before I was afflicted I went astray, but now I obey your word. You are good, and what you do is good; teach me your decrees."

Psalm 119:67–68 (NIV)

5. God Speaks Through His Creation

"The heavens declare the glory of God ... day after day they pour forth speech; night after night they display knowledge."

Psalm 19:1–2

6. God Speaks Through Circumstances

"And we know that God causes everything to work together for the good of those who love God and are called according to his purpose for them."

Romans 8:28 (NLT)

7. God Speaks Through Angels

"Angels are only servants, spirits sent to care for people who inherit salvation."

Hebrews 1:14 (NLT)

8. God Speaks to Us By Giving Us Blessings

"Every good and perfect gift is from above, coming down from the Father."

James 1:17 (NIV)

ACCURACY TEST:

Do your impressions agree with the Scriptures?

HOW TO RECEIVE PERSONAL GUIDANCE FROM GOD

*"I will stand at my watch and station myself on the ramparts;
I will look to see what he will say to me…"*

Habakkuk 2:1

Withdraw: Find a place of solitude

"Jesus often withdrew to lonely places and prayed."

Luke 5:16

Wait: Relax your thoughts and emotions

"Be still in the presence of the Lord, and wait patiently for him to act."

Psalm 37:7 (NLT)

"Be still, and know that I am God."

Psalm 46:10

Watch: Invite God to speak to you
"I will look to see what he will say to me…"

Habakkuk 2:1

"I pray also that the eyes of your heart may be enlightened in order that you may know the hope to which he has called you…"

Ephesians 1:18

Weed: Keep the garden of your heart clean
"If I had not confessed the sin in my heart, the Lord would not have listened. But God did listen!"

Psalm 66:18–19 (NLT)

Write: Record your conversation with the Lord
"Then the Lord replied: 'Write down the revelation…"

Habakkuk 2:2

"This is what the LORD, the God of Israel, says: 'Write in a book all the words I have spoken to you.'"

Jeremiah 30:2

Worship: Let God know you love him
"LORD, I have heard of your fame; I stand in awe of your deeds…"

Habakkuk 3:2

Steps to Follow in the Use of Your Prayer Journal

STEP 1: Find a special place where you can spend quality time with the Lord. Be sure to bring along your Bible, journal, highlighter, and pen.

STEP 2: Read your Bible passage. Choose a book of the Bible through which you will read. (Begin in a New Testament book.) As you read a paragraph or chapter, underline anything the Lord impresses on you as a personal word of insight. Be assured that the Spirit will speak to you through God's Word.

STEP 3: When the Lord has highlighted a special life lesson to you, turn to a new page in your Prayer. Journal to record the following:

Enter the date and Scripture of the day.

Enter the Theme/Topic that described your life lesson.

Enter Yesterday's Highlights

Write out your Key Scripture verse(s).

Record the special insight for living that you have discovered. What do you learn in this section about God, Jesus, or the Holy Spirit?
Is there a warning to heed?
Is there a sin to confess?
Is there an invitation to receive?
Is there an encouragement for me?
Is there an attitude to follow?
These become your insights for living for the day.

Write out a prayer. You may want to learn how to enter into a dialogue with the Lord. For example, after you write a sentence to the Lord, listen to what the Spirit impresses on your heart. Write this out as well. Be sure to do this in the "First Person".

STEP 4: Turn to the Table of Theme Highlights. Record the date, Scripture, theme, and page of the Prayer Journal entries you want to particularly remember (see illustration, Appendix 1)

STEP 5: Complete your devotions by focusing on your Prayer List and your Prayer Jogging Course found on the last page of this book.

List current prayer needs and answers (Appendix 2)

Prayer Jogging Course (Appendix 3)

In the squares provided record names of people you will pray for on a daily and/or weekly basis.

How will you pray for them? Pray the "insight" the Lord gave you in your Bible reading into the lives of those listed in your Prayer Jogging Course for that day. This way you can develop a more consistent prayer ministry.

OVERCOMING THE BARRIERS IN JOURNALING

1. Vision: Look forward to spending personal time with your Heavenly Father. Discover the Joy in Journaling.

2. Missed A Day: Just start up where you left off. Don't let a missed day or two discourage you.

3. Time: If you are married, communicate your "Journal Time" with your spouse. If you are single, share your progress in this discipline with a friend. This will also help you be accountable.

4. It's Too Complicated: Keep it on a level that makes sense to you.

5. It's Too Simple: The written focused insights & Prayers go deep in connecting with God.

Connecting with God (Sample)

DATE: 5/20/2007   **THEME:** Being Perfect

YESTERDAYS HIGHLIGHTS

(You can choose to simply list things you did, persons you met, lessons you learned or events you participated in. Often a little story that occurred to you is worth writing down. You will find that in years to come it will be a delight to read these vignettes that help you to recall the various ordinary days of your life.)

SCRIPTURE

Matthew 5:38–48
Verse for Today Matthew 5:48, "But you are to be perfect, even as your Father in heaven is perfect."

INSIGHT

My father's command for me is to be holy and this really raises the bar of my understanding of His expectations of me. "Perfect" carries the idea of being mature or complete. But God never asks me to do something that is impossible. So becoming perfect means being like Christ through His forgiveness and gift of holiness in my life. It is then that God sees me as perfect through the lens of Jesus Christ who has become my Saviour.

PRAYER

"Abba Father, I hear your call to holiness in my life. Forgive me my sins, yes, also my hidden sins. Give me your gift of holiness and forgiveness moment by moment, hour by hour, and experience by experience."

(Voice of God) Yes my son/daughter, you have understood my call to you. By my indwelling Spirit I will also give you a passion for holiness. As you grow in perfection you will also see me more clearly. I am reminding you of a verse you read yesterday, "God blesses those whose hearts are pure, for they will see God" (Matt. 5:8 NLT).

(The writer) Father, open my eyes that I might see you and worship you will all my heart, mind and strength.
In Jesus' name

Connecting with God

DATE: **THEME:**

YESTERDAY'S HIGHLIGHTS

_____

_____

_____

_____

_____

SCRIPTURE

_____

_____

_____

_____

_____

INSIGHT

_____

_____

_____

_____

_____

PRAYER

_____

_____

_____

_____

_____

Connecting with God

DATE: **THEME:**

YESTERDAY'S HIGHLIGHTS

_____
_____
_____
_____
_____

SCRIPTURE

_____
_____
_____
_____
_____

INSIGHT

_____
_____
_____
_____
_____

PRAYER

_____
_____
_____
_____
_____

Connecting with God

DATE: **THEME:**

YESTERDAY'S HIGHLIGHTS

_____
_____
_____
_____
_____

SCRIPTURE

_____
_____
_____
_____

INSIGHT

_____
_____
_____
_____

PRAYER

_____
_____
_____
_____
_____

Table of Theme Highlights (Sample)

DATE	SCRIPTURE	THEME/TOPIC	PAGE
5/20/2007	Matthew 5:48	Being Perfect	1

Table of Theme Highlights

DATE	SCRIPTURE	THEME/TOPIC	PAGE

Table of Theme Highlights

DATE	SCRIPTURE	THEME/TOPIC	PAGE

Prayer Requests (Sample)

DATE	REQUEST	ANSWERED
5/20/2007	Help me to begin journaling	10/2/2007

Prayer Requests

DATE	REQUEST	ANSWERED

Prayer Jogging Course

AREAS	SUNDAY	MONDAY	TUESDAY	WEDNESDAY	THURSDAY	FRIDAY	SATURDAY
FAMILY							
CHURCH LEADERS							
MISSION-ARIES							
FRIENDS							
UNSAVED							
GOV'T LEADERS							
OTHERS							

Notes

1. An Invitation to Listening to God

1. Gordon MacDonald, *Ordering Your Private World* (Nashville: Thomas Nelson Publishers, 1984), 139.
2. Charles R. Swindoll, *Intimacy with the Almighty* (Vancouver: Word, 1996), 6.
3. MacDonald, 138.
4. Bill Hybels, *Too Busy Not to Pray: Slowing Down to Be with God* (Downers Grove: Intervarsity Press, 1988), 99.
5. Ibid., 100.

2. Learning to Recognize God's Voice

1. Charles Stanley, *How to Listen to God* (Nashville: Thomas Nelson Publishers, 1985), 44.
2. St. Francis de Sales, *Introduction to the Devout Life*, trans. John K. Ryan (Garden City, NY: Doubleday, 1957), 106.
3. Thomas R. Kelly, *A Testament of Devotion, A Testament of Devotion* (New York: Harper & Brothers, 1941), 115.
4. A. W. Tozer, *The Pursuit of God* (Harrisburg, Penn.: Christian Publications, Inc. 1982), 80.

3. Primary Ways God Speaks to Us

1. Richard Foster, *Celebration of Discipline: The Path to Spiritual Growth* (San Francisco: Harper & Row, Publishers, 1978), 30.
2. Oswald Chambers, *Prayer: A Holy Occupation*, Harry Verploegh, ed. (Grand Rapids: Discovery House Publishers, 1992), 12.
3. Bill Hybels, *Too Busy Not to Pray: Slowing Down to be with God*, LaVonne Neff, ed. (Downers Grove: Intervarsity Press, 1988), 94.
4. Summary of an e-mail message sent from Kevin Peters.
5. Henry and Richard Blackaby, *Hearing God's Voice* (Nashville: Broadman & Holman Publishers, 2002), 18.
6. C. Peter Wagner, *Praying with Power: How to Pray Effectively and Hear Clearly from God* (Ventura: Regal Books, 1997), 38.

4. GOD SPEAKS TO US THROUGH THE BIBLE

1. A. W. Tozer, *The Pursuit of God* (Harrisburg, Penn.: Christian Publications, Inc. 1982), 83.
2. Charles Stanley, *Listening to God: Experience a deeper relationship with God by learning to hear His voice* (Nashville: Thomas Nelson Publishers, 1996), 34.
3. Henry and Richard Blackaby, *Hearing God's Voice* (Nashville: Broadman & Holman Publishers, 2002), 98.
4. Ibid., 90–91.
5. Adapted from M. Robert Mulholland Jr., *Shaped by the Word* (Nashville: The Upper Room, 1985), 41–60.

5. GOD SPEAKS THROUGH IMPRESSIONS OF THE HOLY SPIRIT

1. Brother Lawrence, *The Practice of the Presence of God* (Old Tappan, NJ: Revell, 1958), 37–38.
2. Steven Fry, *I Am: The Unveiling of God* (Sisters, Ore.: Multnomah Publishers, 2000), 136–137.
3. C. S. Lewis, *The Weight of Glory and Other Addresses* (Grand Rapids: Eerdmans, 1965), 1–2.

6. GOD SPEAKS TO US THROUGH PEOPLE

1. Dallas Willard, *Hearing God: Developing a Conversational Relationship with God* (Downers Grove: Intervarsity Press, 1999), 17.

7. GOD SPEAKS TO US THROUGH DIFFICULTIES

1. C. S. Lewis, *The Problem of Pain* (Great Britain: Collins Clear-Type Press, 1940), 81.
2. Rachel Naomi Remen, MD, *My Grandfather's Blessings: Stories of Strength, Refuge, and Belonging* (New York: Riverhead Books, 2000), 140–141.

8. GOD SPEAKS TO US THROUGH HIS CREATION

1. Elizabeth Barrett Browning, *Aurora Leigh*, book VII, line 820.
2. Grant R. Jeffrey, *Creation: Remarkable Evidence of God's Design* (Toronto: Frontier Research Publications, 2003), 15.
3. Song by C. Austin Miles.

9. GOD SPEAKS TO US THROUGH CIRCUMSTANCES

1. Henry and Richard Blackaby, *Hearing God's Voice* (Nashville: Broadman & Holman Publishers, 2002), 152.

10. GOD SPEAKS TO US THROUGH ANGELS

1. Billy Graham, *Angels: God's Secret Agents* (Nashville: W. Publishing Group, a Division of Thomas Nelson Co., 1994), 83.
2. Charles Stanley, *Listening to God: Experience a deeper relationship with God by learning to hear His voice* (Nashville: Thomas Nelson Publishers, 1996), 28–29.
3. Graham, 3–4.
4. Dallas Willard, *Hearing God: Developing a conversational relationship with God* (Downers Grove: Intervarsity Press, 1999), 63.

11. GOD SPEAKS TO US BY GIVING US BLESSINGS

1. St. Augustine.

12. JOURNALING: MY LIFE TRAVELOGUE

1. Marilyn Hontz, *Listening for God* (Wheaton Illinois: Tyndale House Publishers, 2004), 188.